FIRESIDE

THE GREAT INTERNATIONAL PAPER AIRPLANE BOOK

by
JERRY MANDER, GEORGE DIPPEL
and HOWARD GOSSAGE

The official record, analysis, and fly-it-yourself compendium
of high-achievement paper airplanes from the *Scientific American*
1st International Paper Airplane Competition,
held during the winter of '66-'67, an event that has
already taken its proper place in aeronautical history.

Told by the men who were there. (Illustrated and annotated)

A FIRESIDE BOOK
PUBLISHED BY
Simon and Schuster · New York

ISBN 0-671-28991-8
ISBN 0-671-21129-3 Pbk.
Library of Congress Catalog Card Number 68-12169
Manufactured in the United States of America

8   9   10   11   12   13   14
                  30   31   32   33   34   35   36   Pbk.

Dedication

The authors wish to dedicate this manuscript to Capt. Fear God Bascomb, out of New Bedford, Massachusetts, who brought the first known pad of lined 8½" x 11" paper from China on May 1, 1743. It may well be said of Capt. Bascomb that without him, the paper airplane as we know it would not have been possible.

Acknowledgments

Since the conclusion of the 1st International Paper Airplane Competition, the most persistent question that has been asked of authors Gossage, Mander and Dippel (respectively the conceptualizer of the event; the writer of the ads; and the art director) has been this:

"How on Earth did you ever get a responsible, respected magazine like *Scientific American* to go along with such a thing?"

Finally, the true story can be told:

The idea was hatched full-blown during a lunch at a New York restaurant; those present, Howard Gossage, Gerard Piel (Publisher of *Scientific American*) and Stephen Fischer (Assistant to the Publisher of the magazine).

One gentleman said, "Why don't we have a paper airplane competition for the magazine?" Another answered, "Why not?" and embellishments aside, there you have it.

The spirit of the occasion was carried along with Gossage via metal airplane back to his associates Jerry Mander and George Dippel of Shade Tree Corporation in San Francisco, and the rest is history. But before proceeding with that history within these pages, the authors would first of all like to pay tribute to Mr. Piel, who is *often* praised for having built *Scientific American* to its present eminence as one of the few most respected publications in the world, but *not* so often praised for the fact that he has done so without that dreadful self-consciousness which precludes *other* great men and ventures from undertaking a paper airplane competition or the like, at least now and then.

In our experience we have found that the biggest thinkers we have dealt with are the ones *most* willing to support such "frivolous" projects; they are doubtless the ones most capable of understanding the importance of them during such days as we find ourselves living in. To Gerard Piel, then, thank you.

Having done that we would also like to point out that the day-to-day running of such a competition—especially the cataloguing and flight testing of 12,000 entries; the publicity demands deriving therefrom; and the organization of arrangements for such huge subcompetitions as were held by American Airlines and the San Francisco *Chronicle*—is no easy matter. The authors, therefore, are brimming with respect and thankfulness toward Mr. Stephen Fischer and Mr. William Yokel, *Scientific American*'s Airplane Design Coordinator, for shouldering this immense burden without shipping it all out to San Francisco to us, as we were in constant fear they would.

There is little doubt that without these two men, the authors, having created a monster, would have had to flee to refuge in Anguilla, or elsewhere, lest we be forever lost under a mountain of paper airplanes.

The authors and the publishers are grateful to the following persons and institutions:

A. A. Backstrom, Waldridge Bailey, Captain Barnaby, Bibliothèque Nationale, Robert Black, Black Star, D. L. Cairns, Esteban Cordero, John Craig, Joseph W. Dauben, Wanda Dillon, Fretz & Wasmuth Verlag AG (for *Das Kleine Buch vom Papierflugzeug* by Richard Katz), L. Groom, Leo Heisser, Y. Hihomiya, Frederick J. Hooven, Edward E. Keyse, Andrew Kimball, Curtis D. Kissinger, Edmund V. Laitone, Clifford Lang, Library of Congress, Fukuo Misumi, Rev. M. Eugene Mockabee, Musée de L'Air, Nasza Ksiergarnia (for *Duza Ksiazka o Malych Samolotach* by Pawel Elsztein), Jim Noble, William Pain, George Peck, Robyn Reinen, Dennis Rietz, Ben Rose, Frank Rosenberg, Royal Aeronautical Society, Prof. James Sakoda, George S. Schairer, Tim Schisler, Louis W. Schultz, David Segal, Cliff Speck, Ronald R. Thompson, S. J. Tweedie, W. Heffer & Sons Ltd. (for *Paper Aeroplanes* by H. G. G. Herklots), Mark B. Wanzenberg, Wide World Photos Inc., F. D. Woodruff, Mary Sue Wunderlich, Mr. Yolen.

Contents

Preface

IN 1931, W. Heffer & Sons Ltd. of Cambridge, England, published a book of essays called *Paper Aeroplanes* by H. G. G. Herklots. The lead essay in the book is also called "Paper Aeroplanes." It is the only essay in English the authors have ever been able to find on this subject, though it has many historical virtues beyond its uniqueness.

As the reader will note, keeping in mind the year of the essay's publication, it in many ways pioneered the way for this volume. For Herklots, as you will see, is the *first* to complain in print over the dearth of published research on the subject.

It was this very failure in serious scholarship which was also at the root of *Scientific American*'s project. Therefore, when Herklots wrote, "Nowhere in literature is there a long-winded thesis on paper aeroplanes," he anticipated the premise of the 1st International Paper Airplane Competition by no less than 35 years! (See Plate 1.)

(Between the time of Herklots' writings and the events we report in this volume, two other general informa-

tion books have appeared, concerning themselves with less significant aspects of paper airplane theory and design. We refer to: *Duza Ksiazka o Malych Samolotach* by Pawel Elsztein, published by Nasza Ksiergarnia, Warsaw, 1956; and of course Richard Katz's 1933 classic, *Das Kleine Buch vom Papierflugzeug.*)

There were differences, however, between Herklots' method and *Scientific American*'s. Herklots felt, for example, that paper airplanes play their primary role within "the faculty of mental escape in the building up of society and of civilisation."

In this respect, he presents a point of view not in consonance with *Scientific American*'s, which included no such unsafe assumptions in advance of empirical evidence. (The headline of the second *Scientific American* advertisement said, "If We Knew What It Was We Would Learn, It Wouldn't Be Research, Would It?" See Plate 2.)

Herklots also raises the shocking question of prejudice against paper airplane designers. "Even at school I was persecuted for my hobby," he says, though in *his* circle, no one ever laughed at golfers, Ping-Pong players or Rugby athletes.

Before the reader surmises from these statements that Herklots suffered from paranoia, we wish to once again remark that the period was 1931, when England was in the grip of a severe depression. Furthermore, prewar tensions were being felt in increasing degree throughout Europe, reflecting themselves in a tendency to be critical of all forms of free expression.

We know of no such tendency today.

So then, with these preliminary remarks, we will leave the reader to judge Herklots in Herklots' own words.

"In these days, when our universities produce so great a number of industrious and indefatigable researchers into all manner of out-of-the-way subjects, I am a little surprised to discover that no man has written a serious and long-winded thesis, treatise, dissertation or monograph on the part played by the faculty of mental escape in the building up of society and of civilisation. The University of Chicago has lately approved a thesis written by a woman on the all-important subject of dish-washing, but more important and wider things are left unheeded. No one, for instance, has yet written the deplorable history of rice pudding. Nor is this really surprising. Some subjects are too vast for compression into thesis form. Not the most long-winded of our researchers possesses a long enough

wind even to run round the confines of the lands of mental escape. For the history of escape is the history of most of the sins and most of the arts of mankind. The whole of the world sighs constantly for the wings of a dove that it may escape, not necessarily to the desert, but anywhere, so long as it is somewhere else. It is because we would like to change, that we take up cat-burgling or barracking at cricket matches. For this reason we play golf or go to the pictures, or engage in what the Victorians used to call brown studies, or get drunk, or, if we happen to be Kubla Khan, living in Xanadu, decree a stately pleasure dome. Modern civilisation employs hundreds of thousands of paid distractors of the mind who are engaged in creating worlds, fantastic or absurd, strange or terrifying, wherein we may forget the things we have to do tomorrow morning and what So-and-so said to us yesterday afternoon. Philosophical speculations and metaphysical consolations both subserve the same end. Music and art —these are also the wings of the dove whereby we may escape. Mr. Siegfried Sassoon has expressed this well in his last book of poems:

When Selfhood can discern no comfort for its cares,
Whither may I turn but to you whose strength my
    spirit shares?
Where may I find but in you.
Beethoven, Bach, Mozart,
Timeless, eternally true,
Heavens that may hold my heart?

"As for me, when the world goes wrong, when the work I have to do tomorrow morning is especially laborious and when the things that So-and-so said to me yesterday afternoon were peculiarly galling, I seldom turn to any of these things. I turn instead to paper aeroplanes. By paper aeroplanes I do not mean paper darts. Darts are easy to make, but there is little satisfaction to be found in them. You throw them; they go straight; that is all. The paper aeroplane is a very different affair. It is, more accurately, a paper glider. You do not throw it. You let it go—or push it very slightly; and the weight ahead carries it forward, gracefully and gently, like a sea gull coming to rest upon the deck of a ship. A little while ago it was a sheet of notepaper, but now it glides like the fairest of white birds. Yet a perfect flight requires very often an infinitude of patience, a folding and refolding, a shaping and reshaping with the scissors. So far as I can tell, there is only one form of paper dart.

"The variety of paper aeroplanes is almost endless. There are monoplanes and biplanes. There are planes like beetles and there are planes like birds. There are planes that fly swift and straight and there are planes that fly slowly in circles. There are planes that can be made to loop the loop. And there are India paper aeroplanes so small and so delicate that even in a dining room they are swiftly lost to sight.

"And yet, for all this, I am practically a lone flier. There is no annual yearbook of suggested designs. Butchers and bakers and candlestick-makers, anti-vivisectionists, aquarists and pondkeepers, members of the food and cookery and catering world, modern churchmen, and those interested in the utilization of waste material—all these have their own magazines in which they can discuss their problems. But I have never lighted on a copy of *The Paper Aeroplane* in which I can discuss my problems: the problem of elevators, the problem of guidance in the air, the peculiar problems of out-of-door flying, the advisability of the metal paper clips for weighting. And not only am I a lone flier. I am also a persecuted flier. Nobody laughs at golf, nobody laughs at Rugby football; few people laugh nowadays at ping-pong, and whereas men snigger at chess they respect it too. But when my friends discover me trimming the wings of paper aeroplanes they laugh me to scorn. Even at school I was persecuted for my hobby. It was in 1918 and we all had influenza. In the dormitory that had hastily become a sanatorium ward I whiled away many hours of tedium by manufacturing my planes. After a time I grew bolder and flew them from the window into the courtyard below. I was afraid that I might be beaten for this, but punishment came in a subtler form. In a later issue of the school magazine there was a sarcastic note about the disgusting mess created by those who had thrown darts into Wright Senior Quad. Darts! They called my aeroplanes darts. That was the worst of all, a wound cutting deeper far than any beating. Even nowadays I dare not fly my aeroplanes by daytime from the windows of my house into the street below. Public

Opinion would never stand it. Yet sometimes, at night, I turn out the light in my room, creep to the window and open it silently. And while the earth is still I watch my dovelike creations floating afar, or eddying to the ground, braving the wind or finding their way round the corner into the next street. Then I shut the window, draw the curtains, turn on the light, and clean up the disgusting mess in my room.

"This is my complaint—that I have never had a chance. No one supports, helps or advises me. No newspaper offers a big money prize for me to win a competition. No newspaper even placards my adventures—LONE FLIER CROSSES BOLSOVER STREET. Often enough, while I've been watching a play from a seat in the gallery, my heart has leapt up at the thought of paper aeroplanes. With a pair of scissors I would so fashion my programme that it would clear the stalls and alight upon the stage. But again, Public Opinion would be all against it. I would be laughed to scorn or hounded from the place. Two communists were arrested who showered leaflets from the gallery of the House of Commons: I know what would happen to me if I started with paper aeroplanes. And only once have I been to the Albert Hall. There I listened from the balcony to brave words and fine speeches. But there was always one thought at the back of my mind, that came into full consciousness in the lacunae between my enthusiasms—that this was the world's most wonderful place for paper aeroplane flights. Lend me the Albert Hall for a night, and I will show you things.

"Paper aeroplanes of another kind I sometimes make...some, it may be, will catch the wind alight and go sailing across the road, round the corner, and into the wider world beyond. I hope so."

CABINET DES ESTAMPES, BIBLIOTHEQUE NATIONALE

Fig. 1   The Montgolfier brothers' balloon

Introduction

ON DECEMBER 12, 1966, a day that was otherwise a "light news day," there appeared on page 37 of *The New York Times* a full-page advertisement on behalf of Lockheed-California Corporation which suggested that it was an altogether good idea, considering America's situation balance-of-payments-wise, for we the people to push on toward completing development of a supersonic transport plane (SST).

For, if there were no American SST, the ad suggested, speed-eager U.S. airlines would be reduced to buying the Anglo-French Concorde SST, thereby further aggravating the already aggravating balance-of-payments crisis. Nor must we forget the implied consequences of "the Soviet SST (TU-144) which also is in development," as the ad pointed out with ominous restraint.

So much for page 37 of *The New York Times*. We turn now to page 38.

To this day, no one has been able to learn the identity of the man in the composing room at *The New York Times,* December 11, 1966, who arranged that *Scientific American*'s advertisement should appear on the very page behind Lockheed's. *Scientific American* has fielded a number of charges that it had prior knowledge of the Lockheed advertisement, and without question, Lockheed has been accused of arranging that its ad run adjacent to theirs. Both deny any such dealings and ask investigating bodies to ferret elsewhere.

Thus another unsolved mystery enters into the annals of aviation.

By nine o'clock of the 12th, the ordinarily quiet offices of *Scientific American* Publisher Gerard Piel were shoulder deep in newsmen. At 10:30 A.M., Mr. Piel found it necessary to adjourn the press to larger quarters to hold a conference.

He was asked if he had planted a spy in the composing rooms. "No, we hadn't," he said.

He was asked if the competition was a thinly veiled cover to protest the SST development. "We are in favor of science," Mr. Piel answered, throwing a paper airplane.

One newsman wondered if there was implied "a paper airplane gap"

1st International Paper Airplane Competition

SCIENTIFIC AMERICAN primarily concerns itself with what Man is up to these days, and our readership is known for travelling more than that of any other magazine. So it is little wonder we have spent considerable time studying the two designs for the supersonic SST airplane recently announced by Boeing and Lockheed. (See Fig. 1 and Fig. 2.)

Soon we'll all be flying around in thin air at Mach 2.7, i.e., from New York to London in 150 minutes. Quite a prospect!

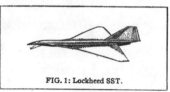

FIG. 1: Lockheed SST.

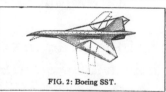

FIG. 2: Boeing SST.

Still, at the close of our inquiry there remained this nagging thought: Hadn't we seen these designs somewhere before?

Of course. Paper airplanes. Fig. 3 and Fig. 4 illustrate only the more classical paper plane designs, in use since the 1920's or so, having a minimum performance capability of 15 feet and four seconds.*

We do not mean to question the men at Boeing and Lockheed, or their use of traditional forms. But it seems

FIG. 3: Paper plane circa 1920, the classic paper plane. Smoothness of flight, grace.

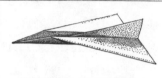

FIG. 4: First developed among paper airplane designers in the 1930's. Known for spectacular darting motions. Note hooked nose.

to us unjust that several million paper plane designers around the world are not also given their due, a credit which if it had been extended some years ago would have saved the pros quite some straining at the drawing boards.

Well anyway, with design having caught up with itself, we can now postulate that there is, right now, flying down some hallway or out of some moviehouse balcony in Brooklyn, the aircraft which will make the SST 30 years obsolete. No?

Consider this: Never since Leonardo da Vinci, the Patron Saint of paper airplanes, has such a wealth of flight research and experimentation remained untouched by cross-disciplinary study and publication. Paper airplane design has become one of those secret pleasures performed behind closed doors. Everybody does it,

but nobody knows what anyone else has learned.

Many's the time we've spied a virtuoso paper plane turn the corner of the office hallway, or suddenly rise up over the desk, or on one occasion

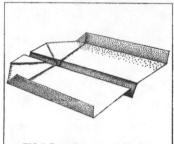

FIG. 5: Drawn from memory, this plane was last seen in 12th floor stairwell at 415 Madison Ave. Do you know its designer? Where is he?

we'll never forget, veer first down the stairs to the left, and suddenly to the right, staying aloft 12 seconds in all. (See Fig. 5.)

But who is its designer? Is he a Board Chairman or a stock boy? And what has he done lately?

All right then. In the interests of filling this information gap, and in light of the possibility that the future of aeronautics may now be flying in a paper plane, we are hereby calling for entries to the 1st International Paper Airplane Competition.

*(In paper plane circles, of course, a *better* time is a *longer* time. If a plane can stay aloft, floating on the air as it were, for 15 seconds, *that* is a virtue, as indeed it was for the Bros. Wright. One would assume that today's commercial designers, who seek planes to get from here to there and *down* as quickly as possible, would not have been much interested in the study of paper planes, or the Bros. Wright. In light of the illustrations, our assumption appears to be wrong.)

Rules

1. Scientific American has created The Leonardo (see Fig. 6) to be winner's trophy in each of these four categories:
a) duration aloft,
b) distance flown,
c) aerobatics, and
d) Origami.

2. A silver Leonardo will go to winners not involved professionally in air travel, and a titanium Leonardo (the metal being used in the SST) to professional entrants, that is, people employed in the air travel

FIG. 6: The Leonardo.

business, people who build non-paper airplanes, and people who subscribe to Scientific American, because they fly so much.

3. Please feel at liberty to rip out this page, fold it, and use it as your official entry. If you find newsprint is not suitable to your particular design, however, use your own paper of any size or description. (Rag content and water marks will not have any bearing on the final decision.) Or, send for your free Official Entry Form Pad—reprints of this ad, padded, which you can stand on your desk, or hang near it, and with which you and your associates can make literally dozens of Official Entries.

4. You may enter as often as you like, being sure to include your *name, address, employer*, if any,

and the *classes* in which you would like your entry to qualify.

5. Send your entry to us, somehow, at this address: Scientific American, Leonardo Trophy Competition, 415 Madison Ave., New York 10017, postmarked by January 16, 1967. On January 21 all entries will be test-flown down our hallways by a panel of distinguished judges whose identity we'll announce at a later date (so as to not influence anyone's design).

6. Except that we will publish scale drawings of the winning designs, all other rights to same remain reserved to the designer. We, however, will do our bit towards assuring immediate production.

Thank you.

Plate 1

as between the Soviet Union and the United States and what the implications of such might be. Another wondered if, as the ad suggested, it were true that the SST designs were actually derivative of classic paper airplane designs, would not that throw all rights to them into "the public do-

BLACK STAR—WERNER WOLFF

Fig. 2 Gerard Piel, Publisher of *Scientific American*, holds paper airplane.

main"? Would it not mean that any group of fly-by-night businessmen could quickly build their own competitive SST after the same design?

It was perhaps due to the prospect of thousands of neighborhood groups home-brewing bathtub SST's that the international press responded with

such enthusiasm to the competition. (See *also* Chapter for further observation on the question of the rights to SST design.)

Within days, editorials supporting the effort were seen in more than a hundred American newspapers. (Surprisingly, dozens of the editorials were exactly the same, word for word, in papers as geographically separate as the Athol (Mass.) *News*, the San Antonio (Texas) *Express*, and the Evansville (Indiana) *Courier*. At first, we passed it off as another startling coincidence. But giving it further thought, we wonder whether there isn't, somewhere, an underground syndicate that provides editorials as the AP and UPI do "hard news"? We find it disturbing somehow to realize that it is possible

ROME, N.Y., SENTINEL

Fame on the Wings of Paper

A full-page advertisement in the Dec. 13 New York Times solemnly detailed the Lockheed-California Co.'s case for building a supersonic transport, or SST. On the next page, an ad similar in appearance to Lockheed's announced the Scientific American's First International Paper Airplane Competition. Thus do the sublime and the ridiculous coexist, even though it is not easy in this instance to tell which is which.

The ordinarily staid Scientific American was struck, it said, by the resemblance of proposed SST airframe designs to those of paper airplanes. The magazine reasoned it was "unjust" that paper airplane builders had not been given their due, "a credit which if it had been extended some years ago would have saved the pros quite same straining at the drawing boards." Entries — thousands of them — were to have been test-flown in the hallways of the Scientific American's New York offices on Jan. 21. But response to the contest was so overwhelming that the fly-off date had to be moved back to Feb. 14. A "panel of distinguished

judges" will determine the w which then will be duplicated sheeted brass and flown in w smoke tunnels of Princeton sity.

"Never since Leonardo d the Patron Saint of paper a has such a wealth of flight and experimentation rema touched by cross-disciplina and publication," the American asserts. If this p accepted, it is only fitting t winners in the paper airp test should be awarded trop ed Leonardos. Entries will in four categories: (1) dura (2) distance flown, (3) a and (4) origami (the art of paper folding).

While the contest ma frivolous, it could produce formation of scientific valu on Mackenzie, director o seum of Art. Science and Briodeprgt, Conn., wants the winning entries in gallery. Mackenzie could that everyone laughed at Wilbur Wright, too.

Fig. 3

that the editorial of the South Croupier (Nevada) *News* is not written, after all, by a thin man with a green visor, but by a New York angle-shooter. But then, that's the subject of another book entirely.)

Abroad, news magazines and papers responded with some mixture of dismay, enthusiasm and delight at this latest venture in American fancy. The politically middle-of-the-road Paris daily *France-Soir,* for example, cheered the development:

"We await with impatience the results of these first investigations....It is in any case good news; perfectly illustrative of certain typically American qualities—ingeniousness, ingenuousness, a sense of humor and straightforwardness."

But the left-wing *Nouvel Observateur,* often critical of the military implications of American aerospace achievements, was more cautious in its response, only reporting the facts of the event, preferring perhaps to see if the winning paper plane was converted immediately to military uses.

The Australian press ignored the political implication of the event and got right down to paper airplanes. At least three of Australia's dailies undertook competitive competitions— two for paper airplanes, and one, *The Australian,* created something called a "Paper Bootbox, Biscuit Barrel, Whatever Contest," surpassed in obscurity of meaning only by Andy Warhol's "Water Bomb Competition"

presented in the New York *World Journal Tribune.*

By the end of the competition, more than thirty-five pounds of news clippings were collected (a stack roughly three feet square by four feet high, after scissor-clipping) and as *Scientific American*'s summary ad indicated, the final fly-offs were covered by a television and press corps equaled in size only by the visit of Pope Paul to New York. (*See* Fig. 4.)

Twelve thousand entries came in, almost every one with a lengthy letter attached giving detailed instructions to whoever was to throw it and providing notes on the significance of the particular design. Some of these letters are quoted in Appendix I, entitled "Letters," but all of them, suffice it to say, were marked by a devotion to cause that was moving in its sincerity.

As a further indication of the enthusiasm of respondents, it is worth noting that the problem of how to physically get one's paper plane through the mails to *Scientific American* required a certain amount of time, energy, and ingenuity. The entrants solved the problem each in his own way. Some were mailed with 5c stamps affixed to the nose (with little apparent effect on aerodynamic characteristics); others in cardboard tubes, airplane hangar-like boxes, styrofoam concoctions, coffee cans, plastic boxes, shoe boxes, cigar boxes, candy boxes, 1-gallon milk cartons, a 6-foot-long metal cylinder, and—by far the largest

Fig. 4   The assembled press observes the Final Fly-offs; New York Hall of Science; the morning of Washington's Birthday Eve, 1967.

number—in cereal boxes of no determinable brand preference. (From *Scientific American* to the testing grounds, all entries were taken by car.)

Before the competition was completed, subcompetitions had been set up by hundreds of grade schools and high schools around the country, a number of colleges including Columbia and Harvard, by Lockheed, Grumman, and Douglas Aircraft corporations, by members of the science staff of the British Embassy in Washington, by American Airlines, which held subcompetitions in every city it serves, and by any number of newspapers, including the London *Daily Sketch,*

the West Yellowstone (Montana) *Wretched Mess News,* and the Newhall (California) *Register.* More than 3,000 entries were submitted by the San Francisco *Chronicle* alone.

The *Chronicle*'s Executive Editor, Mr. Scott Newhall, as soon as he saw the first ad, wired to Piel offering to serve as West Coast depository for the planes. The very next day the paper featured the story in an 8-column banner head (see Fig. 5), and assigned its science reporter, David Perlman, to follow developments as they broke.

Perlman, a crack researcher, within five days had made several startling discoveries with respect to the role of paper airplanes in the history of aero-

[19]

nautics and dutifully reported them to his readers:

"Vittorio Sarti of Italy in 1828 designed a genetic hybrid between a sailboat and a helicopter with great vanes of paper designed to catch soaring breezes. It never got beyond drawing paper. (See Fig. 6.)

"But in 1847 Werner Siemens, a German Army officer and student of aerial navigation, designed the world's first rocket plane, propelled by gunpowder. Its tail resembled common contemporary versions of paper gliders. (See Fig. 7.)

"An albatross inspired France's Jean-Marie Le Bris to build his glider in 1868. It was launched from a cart drawn by a galloping horse. (See Fig. 8.) Note the plane's needle nose, direct

ancestor of today's supersonic concepts.

"A brilliant success was Octave Chanute's biplane glider of 1896, here piloted gracefully by A. M. Herring, who ran down a hill to take off." (See Fig. 9.)

Perlman, questioned repeatedly, refused to reveal his sources for much of this research except to say that "some nice middle-aged lady in the Science section of the Public Library [San Francisco] was very helpful." Nor did he reveal the source for a later discovery concerning another phase of paper airplaning—origami.

(The *Chronicle* stated that this art dates "to the early Heian Era—782 to 1184 A. D." It reported that small fan-like paper planes were constructed of wood and thin paper and were

Fig. 5

SAN FRANCISCO CHRONICLE

PAPER AIRPLANES --- A GLOBAL TEST

Scientific American reports this unusual model was found in a stairwell. Its designer is unknown.

THE WEATHER
Bay Area: Fair except for patches of morning fog; little temperature change. High Thursday, 55 to 60; low, 40 to 50. Gentle winds. See Page 43.

San Francisco Chronicle
THE VOICE OF THE WEST

★★★★ **FINAL**

102nd Year No. 349   CCCCAAA   THURSDAY, DECEMBER 15, 1966   10 CENTS ⬤ GArfield 1-1111

An International Search
For Best Paper Airplane

*Chronicle Joins Unique
Quest for Great Designs*

By David Perlman
Science Correspondent

The San Francisco Chronicle announced yesterday it is proud to support the First International Paper Airplane Competition throughout the West Coast of the United States and all the nations of the vast Pacific Basin.

The competition was launched

Lockheed SS-

"IF WE KNEW WHAT IT WAS WE WOULD LEARN, IT JUST WOULDN'T BE RESEARCH, WOULD IT?"

Professor DAVID C. HAZEN, *Princeton University*

BULLETIN: At the request of Origami entrants, whose folding can get very complicated, and entrants from abroad, whose planes are mostly coming by ship, Scientific American has extended the 1st International Paper Airplane Competition deadline to February 14, Valentine's Day. (Hearts, paper frills and tender sentiments will not, however, influence the decision of the judges.)

SYNOPSIS

SOME WEEKS AGO, noting the similarity between the classical paper airplane delta wing model, circa 1920, and the supersonic SST airplane designs, Scientific American launched the first formal inquiry into paper airplane design. (See typical SST below.)

We felt that if paper airplane designers were doing, four decades ago, what commercial designers have just got around to, then we should learn if there's not by now, darting and swooping and gliding its way through the hallways of America, the SST of the year 2,000.

We certainly do not wish to suggest that the commercial designs are directly derivative, which, if it were so, would put them "in the Public Domain." Nor

Typical SST. See also typical paper plane. Note similarity.

do we mean to imply "a paper airplane gap," as one news reporter has put it, "between America and the Soviet Union."

INFORMATION VOID

We are just doing our bit towards filling an information void that has frustrated paper airplane designers since the inception of papyrus. Lacking any cross-disciplinary knowledge as to their colleagues' findings and despite official indifference, they have privately continued their daily experiments with lift co-efficient applications; in offices, backyards and from suburban rooftops. And somehow, they have (apparently) managed to be the major influence on the shape of planes today.

THE JUDGING

Well, the Dark Ages of research have passed. Why, after all, should science any longer be dependent upon accidental sightings of anonymously launched aircraft from down the block or across the hall?

The time has come for this wealth of uncatalogued knowledge, bearing upon the frontiers of our age, to be collected and published.

At the right, you see seven men and one woman, each a pioneer in some aspect of aerodynamic principle or design, whose fingertips will launch the fruits of what was heretofore the underground of aircraft design.

The judging will be two-phased:

1) All entries will be flown down the corridors of Scientific American.

The halls are basic New York-office-building-type; the longest is eighty feet, the highest is twelve feet, and the widest is ten feet. Should your entry be thwarted by these dimensions, a large nearby lobby is also available.

We regret it will be impossible for entrants to fly their own planes as has been requested. Our judges will, however, be pleased to follow projection in-

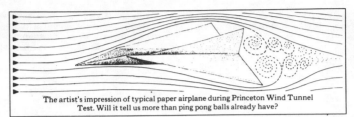

The artist's impression of typical paper airplane during Princeton Wind Tunnel Test. Will it tell us more than ping pong balls already have?

structions you may enclose. (It is only pertinent to add this: If in order to fly properly, your entry requires *you* to do the launching each time, this would seem to call into question the inherent objective validity of the design.)

2) Following the hallways test, those entries still in the running will be taken to Princeton University, where a special balancing mechanism has been devised; one capable of testing paper airplanes for basic aerodynamics within the Princeton Wind Tunnel. (Entries in the Origami sections will be spared this more strenuous exercise.)

PING PONG BALLS

What our judges will learn, no one can say, but there is this startling news: Recent research at Princeton on ping pong balls has indicated an apparent similarity as to flight characteristics

between these *low* speed objects, and *hyper*sonic Mach 20 aircraft attempting to safely negotiate the difficult re-entry and landing procedure. "By now," Professor Hazen reports, "we know more about the aerodynamics of ping pong balls than anyone else in the world."

Now who would have thought, in this age when the primary virtue is the getting from here to there as *quickly* as possible, that the testing of *low* speed objects could have such profound importance?

Well, that's the point of all this. There's little enough chance for any of us to really get on the inside of things these days so let's just proceed as though the world of aviation and space travel is a book with blank pages and we are in charge of the text. (Or shall we merely rip them out, fold, and fly?) Thank you.

PANEL OF JUDGES: SCIENTIFIC AMERICAN 1ST INTERNATIONAL PAPER-AIRPLANE COMPETITION. *(In alphabetical order)*

MR. SURENDRA BAHADUR
President, Go Fly A Kite Store, New York City; one of few men in the world to have flown a kite to upwards of 4,000 feet.

CAPT. LEE CERMAK
Pilot-In-Charge, Goodyear Blimp ("The Mayflower")*

MRS. SUSAN CLEMENTS
U. S. Women's Skydiving Style Champion, 1964, 1965, 1966 (in which parachutist does 360 turns and two backflops in shortest time possible); Women's Overall Champion, 1965; veteran, at age 22, of 470 jumps.**

PROF. DAVID C. HAZEN,
Assoc. Dean of Faculty, Princeton University; member, Dept. of Aerospace and Mechanical Sciences; pioneer researcher in low-speed flight at Princeton Subsonic Aerodynamics Lab.

PROF. EDMUND V. LAITONE
Chairman, Aeronautical Sciences Div., Univ. of California, Berkeley; former member Nat'l Advisory Committee for Aeronautics (NACA), specialist in high speed aerodynamics; former Section Head, Flight Research Engineering, Cornell Aeronautical Lab.

MAJOR S. S. PIKE
President, Skywriting Corporation of America; inventor of precision 5-plane Sky-Typing; supervisor of skywriting project which brought the name Pepsi-Cola to 8,000 cities and towns, 160,000 times.

CDR. R. E. SCHREDER
U. S. National Soaring Champion 1958, 1960, 1966; holder of three world speed records for gliders; designer and builder of 14 aircraft, both sailplane and powered types; member of Helms Soaring Hall of Fame.

MR. BUNJI TAGAWA
Sage Fellow in Philosophy, Cornell University; prominent technical illustrator; Instructor in Origami, P.S. 29, New York.

*The word blimp, according to Goodyear, is not derived from the descriptive phrase "Balloon, Type B, limp" as has been suggested from time to time, but in fact dates to 1915 when a certain Lt. Cunningham of the British air forces became amused at

the sound he heard on the occasion of flipping his thumb at the gasbag.
**Mrs. Clements reports that the U. S. has 20,000 sky divers, and the Soviet Union .3 million. Does this suggest a skydiving gap?

Plate 2

1st International Paper Airplane Competition; A Last Backward Glance

Fig. 1. Six members of the Panel of Jurors at the 1st International Paper Airplane Competition shown during Final Flyoffs observing one of 43 finalists launched for their study and the press. The particular entry they are watching was entered in the distance category, and flew some 87 feet before crashing into a CBS camera, at one foot three inches above ground. It was reflown.

By now, most of you are acquainted with the names, performances and other details of the Final Flyoffs held Washington's Birthday Eve at the New York Hall of Science. (As one news account put it, the event "drew international press coverage not seen since the visit of Pope Paul.")

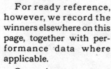

Fig. 2. The Leonardo. Proud possession of 7 winners whose paper planes were judged best of 11,851 entries.

For ready reference, however, we record the winners elsewhere on this page, together with performance data where applicable.

Our *primary* purpose now, is to review with you what we have learned from this experiment.

This much *is* certain. At long last the hitherto uncelebrated and uncatalogued achievements of aircraft design's "underground" have had their day in the sky.

And, there's this: A mere eight weeks after our competition was formally announced the long lost notebooks of Leonardo da Vinci, the Patron

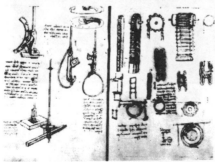

Fig. 3. Two pages of drawings by Leonardo da Vinci, Patron Saint of Paper Airplanes, discovered eight weeks after competition was announced. This development alone is said to have made the entire project worthwhile.

Saint of Paper Airplanes, whose name graces our winner's trophy (see Fig. 2 and Fig. 3), were suddenly discovered.

If no further benefit accrued to science during this project, would not this discovery be ample?

But, going on....

One of our distinguished panel of jurors, Prof.

David Hazen of Princeton's Aeronautics Dept., when asked if indeed we *had* found the key to the SST of the year 2000 flying about in a paper airplane, stated categorically, "No, we have learned nothing new at all."

BERKELEY PROTEST

Not wishing to excite controversy within academia, we must yet observe that another juror, Prof. Edmund Laitone of Berkeley protested, believing Prof. Hazen may have spoken hastily.

Fig. 4. Entry from Mr. P. W. Swift of Xerox Corp., considered by Prof. Edmund Laitone, Chairman of the Aeronautics Dept. at the Univ. of California, Berkeley, so interesting aerodynamically, as to warrant "serious additional study."

Several of the entries need further study, Prof. Laitone indicated, particularly one dart-like object distinguished by flight-perpendicular ring air foils (hoops) both forward and aft. (See Fig. 4.) Prof. Laitone felt "it raises important questions concerning an aspect of aerodynamics that has had virtually no study."

"I would like to know," he added, "exactly what the optimum diameter-length ratio for cylindrical lifting surfaces would be at various Mach and Reynolds numbers? We may find it demonstrates lift characteristics and stability potentials applicable to *both* supersonic and subsonic speeds."

An exciting prospect to be sure.

And now on to the statistical data.

U. S. GOVERNMENT

In all, 5,144 people entered 11,851 airplanes. They came from 28 countries including Liberia and Switzerland, though the largest number of foreign entries were from Japan (some 750), mostly in origami categories. The U. S. government, while not admitting that it considered the winning of this competition vital to national interests, was represented by entries from 18 of its agencies.

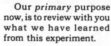

Fig. 5. Actual size study of smallest entry. Entered in the distance category with instructions to drop straight down from upstretched hand. It was decided, however, that distance would be judged on horizontal rather than downward vertical, as that measure would be limited by the inherent size of the individual dropping it. Furthermore, entry was discovered to be made from foil, not paper.

The smallest entry received measured .08 x .00003 inches (see Fig. 5) submitted by the Space Particles and Field Dept. of Aerospace Corp. The largest entry was 11 feet. Entered in the distance flown category, it flew two times its length.

DR. SAKODA

The most interesting statistic, we believe, is that against an estimated 5,000 entries from children, the seven winners were all grownups and between them have devoted 314 years to paper airplane design and experimentation. All seven are engaged in science and engineering, even the ori-

gami winner, Dr. James Sakoda, a professor of anthropology who specializes in computer programming.

Frederick Hooven, of Ford, whose flying wing (see Fig. 6) won in duration aloft, learned his aerodynamics as a student of Orville Wright's, using Mr. Wright's own wind tunnel for early testing.

And Capt. R. S. Barnaby, an aerobatics winner, was founder of the N. Y. Model Aero Club back in 1909.

ENGLAND, 1934

Captain Barnaby presented us with the startling news that the very model that won him first place in our competition won him second place in a paper plane competition in England, 1934.

Does this suggest that aerodynamics has retrogressed over the years? It is hard to say since who knows *what* won first place in '34?

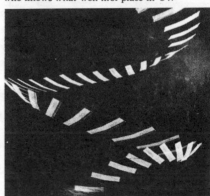

Fig. 6. Flying wing which won duration aloft category. It is shown here in stroboscopic illumination taken at 17 images per second.

You see, without continuously available data, we have merely our imaginations to guide us, which brings us to this special good news:

Commander Richard Schreder, another of our jury who is also national Soaring Champion, has suggested that the American Soaring Society will be pleased to keep our effort aloft, as it were, by sponsoring the 2nd International Paper Airplane Competition, a suggestion we heartily endorse.

For, even as a magazine whose readership is devoted to technological advance and for whom air travel is a way of daily life, we still remain convinced that there is a world of discovery, pleasure and satisfaction in all manner of subsonic activity, from the walking through forests to the flying of paper airplanes. Or as Capt. Lee Cermak, still another of our judges and pilot of the Goodyear blimp Mayflower put it:

"I don't care how much you fly, you won't ever see a jet stop, just to take a better look at the sharks."

WINNERS OF THE LEONARDO

Duration aloft Nonprofessional*	Jerry A. Brinkman Assistant Sales Manager Globe Industries, Dayton, Ohio	9.9 seconds aloft	Aerobatics Nonprofessional	Edward L. Ralston, University of Illinois, (and Clark, Dietz & Associates, Consulting Engineers) Urbana, Illinois
Duration aloft Professional**	Frederick Hooven, Special Consultant to the General Manager, Ford Motor Co., Detroit	10.2 seconds aloft	Aerobatics Professional	Capt. R. S. Barnaby, USN (Ret.), Exhibits Consultant to the Director, Science Museum, Franklin Institute, Philadelphia, Penn.
Distance flown Nonprofessional	Louis W. Schultz, Engineering Group Manager, Stewart Warner Corp., Oak Brook, Illinois	58 feet, 2 inches	Origami Nonprofessional	Prof. James Sakoda, Professor of Sociology and Anthropology, Brown University, Providence, Rhode Island
Distance flown Professional	Robert B. Meuser, Lawrence Radiation Lab., Univ. of California, Berkeley	91 feet, 6 inches (At this point, while still aloft entry hit rear wall of Hall of Science.)	Origami Professional	The judges did not consider that any entry in this category was worthy of The Leonardo.

NOTE: All entries were pre-tested by students of the NASA Goddard Inst. of Space Studies who reported that entries performed considerably better in preliminary testing than in the finals. The reason for this was not nervousness before the judges, but rather that the TV lights created severe thermals invariably hazardous to paper plane flight.

*"Nonprofessionals" were defined in our rules as those not involved professionally in air travel.

°°"Professionals" were defined as "people employed in the air travel business, people who build non-paper airplanes, and people who subscribe to Scientific American, because they fly so much."

° SCIENTIFIC AMERICAN, 1967.

Plate 3

Fig. 6   Sarti's device

equipped "with a fairly heavy, sharp or blunt object on the nose and were used in battle around around 700 A.D. according to some historians.")

Nonetheless, we owe a vote of thanks to the *Chronicle,* and to Perlman himself, for these valued findings. Having done that, we may ask what else has been learned?

Immediately following the Final Fly-offs at the New York Hall of Sci-

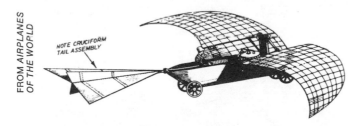

NOTE CRUCIFORM TAIL ASSEMBLY

Fig. 7   Siemen's rocket plane

Fig. 8   Le Bris's glider

Fig. 9   Chanute's biplane

ence, an academic debate developed between the two aeronautical scientists on the jury.

As Plate 3 suggests, Professor David Hazen of Princeton University felt the entries to the competition revealed nothing at all. This opinion, however, was vigorously opposed by Professor Edmund V. Laitone of the University of California at Berkeley who had high hopes for one entry in particular, a ring air foil model submitted by an employee of the Xerox corporation. (See Special Added Chapter.)

As we go to press with this edition, it is some five months since the competition has concluded and Professor Laitone has delightedly revealed to Mr. Piel that indeed scientific knowledge may have been furthered measurably.

In a letter dated May 29, 1967, and which has already been placed in *Scientific American*'s archives, Professor Laitone revealed this: "I, for one, certainly enjoyed the contest and learned some interesting new things."

Laitone didn't stop there. Following the suggestions of one of the winners, Mr. Frederick Hooven, he is proceeding on the researching of flying wings of paper begun by none other than Orville Wright.

A particularly startling and unexpected aspect of the research, according to Laitone, is that "in order to conduct these tests we have had to develop a very accurate wind tunnel balance that can simultaneously measure the lift and drag of a model to an accuracy of 1/10th gram, or 0.0035 oz. This in itself," he pointed out, is interesting, "…because we constructed this extremely accurate balance at practically no cost and very little effort, by utilizing the mechanical parts from a war-surplus aircraft auto pilot.

"As far as we know," Laitone continued on the subject of his wind tunnel balance, "the accuracy we obtained of 1/10th gram is more than ten times more sensitive than any wind tunnel balance we have ever heard of."

Congratulations, sir!

But what about the planes themselves? Well, even in this day of supersonic flight, not every answer is obtainable at first blush. Professor Laitone's work on the ring air foil model from Xerox continues without interruption and he promises news of its achievements in the future. For that moment, we, as you, wait with eager hearts.

Brief Annotated History
of Aeronautics

BEFORE PUSHING ON into the Introduction, Appendices, et cetera, the authors wish to place the extraordinary developments of '66 and '67 into the perspective of aeronautical history. We have therefore engaged in a limited research effort, the findings of which we present for you here, with appropriate annotations.

The history of aeronautics dates clear back to the ancients, when "observers of the flight of birds and of projectiles stirred speculation as to the forces involved and the manner of their interaction. These speculations, however, were in general carried on without benefit of what has become known as the 'experimental method.'"[1]

Skipping on up to 1250, we find Roger Bacon making the first printed suggestion for a gas-filled balloon that could carry a man. But it took Leonardo da Vinci to determine that air offered resistance to the movement of a solid object, though he believed air compression was the key to loft. He thought, for example, that the rapid flapping of birds' wings created a region of compressed air beneath the wings, providing the loft.[2]

Nothing could have been further from the truth.

Galileo later established the fact of air resistance and arrived at the conclusion that the resistance was proportional to the velocity of the object passing through it.[3] Then, in the 17th century, a Dutch physicist, Christian Huygens "may have been the first to appreciate that the resistance of air to the motion of a body was proportional to the square of the velocity."[4] Huygens, though, "used an experimental approach. Newton reached the same conclusion by deduction."[5]

"The work of Newton in setting forth the laws of mechanics marked the beginnings of the classical theories of aerodynamics." He discovered that "the pressure acting on the plates that face an air stream is proportional to the product of the density of the air, the area of the plate, the square of the

---

[1]*Encyclopaedia Britannica*. Vol. 1. "A-Antarah," page 824.

[2]*Ibid.*
[3]*Op cit.*
[4]*Ibid.*
[5]*Ibid.*

velocity and the square of the sine of the angle of inclination."[6]

Of course, the rest is implied.

Still it is vital to especially note that the first public launching of a workable aircraft—a hot-air balloon of "showy appearance"[7] — was accomplished on June 5, 1783, by Joseph and Jacques Etienne Montgolfier, *sons of a successful paper maker.** (See Fig. 1.)

Now back to the business of the day; today's paper airplane, its meaning and future in society.

---

[6]*Ibid.*

[7]*Encyclopaedia Britannica,* 11th Edition (Handy Volume Issue). Page 262.

---

*Their experiment, though soon surpassed, had a powerful grab on man's imagination. Even today, "montgolfier" is retained in French argot as a common noun to describe that exquisite, brutalizing, inflated morning-after head.

Prologue

IN TRIBUTE TO
RUFUS PORTER, THE INVENTOR
OF THE AEROPORT

ON ANY NUMBER of counts, Rufus Porter is deserving of special attention in this book.

Not the least important of these to the authors is the fact that in 1845 he founded *Scientific American*, sponsor of the event with which we are dealing.

But equally important, surely, is that he was himself the inventor of the first self-propelled airship, and more. For, having pondered his new dirigible's implications and realizing, doubtless, that it is not enough to fly—there is also the importance of landing—Mr. Porter surpassed even that achievement by inventing the first "aeroport." It is with no attempt to discredit that we point out that he invented the aeroport for dirigibles, not jets. There was hardly any point in inventing anything that would only be grown over with grass by the time it was used, not to mention the inevitable upkeep costs from 1850 to 1950 when there would be some practical value for such a jetport.

It is also worth adding that on January 23, 1851, Porter very nearly *did* hasten our entry into the Air Age, as on that date he urgently appealed to the Senate for an appropriation of funds to experiment in practical aviation. (Is it possible he had budding jetport plans after all?)

The Senate, however, with the uncanny prescience unique to lawmakers and public officials, was somehow aware that the Air Age was not scheduled to begin officially until a much later date and hence declined to invest in it prematurely. (It is just such invaluable insights that keep history on its orderly course from war to war and prevent us from rushing headlong into an uncertain future.)

Praiseworthy as Porter's aeronautical notions may have been, they would not of themselves occasion this special tribute in a book on paper airplanes. There were, in years past, many other men who left the thumbprints of their genius on the skies. Why then choose Rufus Porter?

Well, why not choose Rufus Porter?

There is little enough question, judging from the way he lived his life, that he was the sort of man who would be pleased about being honored in any book devoted to paper airplanes.

Mr. Porter, to illustrate our point, made no pretense of devoting his life to Science. The very idea would have made him laugh. He devoted his science to Life. That uniquely fulfilling viewpoint enabled him to be in one lifetime a musician, portrait painter, landscape artist, soldier, sailor, dancing master, protean husband and father, religious philosopher, inventor, editor, and a good many other things that have nothing directly to do with paper airplanes.

His given reason for establishing the *Scientific American* was that while there were scores of publications devoted to all sorts of things, there was none "devoted to improvement." Accordingly, he filled its pages with news and notes and commentary on anything and everything that might enrich an individual life or improve the common condition. In a series of articles on painting, for example, he advised the would-be landscape artist, "...it is neither necessary, nor expedient, in all cases, to imitate nature."

In any event, Porter enjoyed exhorting others to "excel nature itself." To create something beautiful even "though not in perfect imitation of anything."

Rufus Porter saw the world as the God-given playground of man and he looked to science to provide the toys. His *Scientific American* had no qualms about including jokes on the front page along with sober-sided technical news. In that spirit, a paper airplane competition could hardly be deemed less worthy than the competition to design an SST.

To Rufus Porter, therefore, thanks and *Godspeed*.

Chapter

There was some talk of omitting the main section of the book altogether except that it seemed fitting to use this otherwise waste space to reflect on What Might Have Been: lost opportunities, their fragile fragrance forever pressed in the center of this massive tome.

First we should like to pay tribute to the men who constituted the backbone of *Scientific American*'s 1st International Paper Airplane Competition: those who never got it off the ground. We refer to the host of *would-be* contestants who read about the competition and thought it was a grand idea. With faces aglow they started to folding anew their accustomed version of the paper airplane—the very model they had brought to perfection in 5th-grade study hall and which had given them solace and relief from corporate tedium through the ensuing years. At last! A chance to match their nonpareil against All Those Others.

There must have been millions of them. If only they had listened to the boy inside, whispering, "My plane can beat your plane!" Of course they didn't.

What they did do, after defeatist grown-up reflecting on it, was wistfully flick their lovechild across the room, smashing it into a blank wall along with their bittersweet dreams of glory.

We think we can reconstruct the logic, perhaps justified (who is now to say?), which prompted this horde of paper kamikazes. After the first fine flush evaporated, they looked on their handiwork with new eyes. That is to say that they felt the eyes of *others* upon it and experienced something akin to stage fright. Why?

Recall that since childhood this had been a secret practice. Now, on submission, *everyone* would know. Suddenly their custom-built wonder became a very poor creature indeed. Besides, one could be sure (the despairing logic went) that, with *Scientific American* sponsoring it, the technical competition would be stiff, quite stiff; some scientific fellow would surely win. This, as we have seen, is exactly what did happen, though what the outcome would have been had the bashful millions ventured forth is hard to imagine.

Enough to say that this eleventh-hour withdrawal, not to say cringing, on the greater part of the very grass roots of paper aircraft design—every man who has ever folded a plane—represents an incalculable loss to the science.

Where did all go wrong? It may have been in the very beginning. Perhaps if the opening announcement of the Competition had been less serious, less scientifically intimidating...

———

In passing, why is it that paper aviation is exclusively a male domain? Has anyone ever known of a paper aviatrix? How many have ever seen a small *girl* scale a paper plane across a classroom or anywhere else? (Of the 12,000 entries to the paper airplane competition, fewer than 1,000 were from women.) Is it a field (like the conducting and composing of music, chess, barbecuing, the humor of W. C. Fields) with which women cannot really cope? Science does not tell us.

———

Of more than passing interest is the failure of anyone to try to establish a verifiable claim to the basic SST design by virtue of priority. In our opinion, the rights to this valuable property could have been authenticated easily. Perhaps they still can, though it is likely that, with *Scientific American*'s competition having come and gone without even one claimant, the delta wing is now in the public domain for

good. Maybe it is just as well, though it is a shame to think of all that royalty money just lying around with nobody getting the good of it.

To have staked out a claim to the basic patent would have been simplicity itself. All one needed to do for starters was be elderly—over 100, say—and present affidavits: from one's principal, Sunday school teacher, etc.

There are, on the face of it, a couple of drawbacks to this straightforward approach, among them: a) A 110-year-older is not as likely to be aggressive in asserting his rights as a person of less mature years might be; b) Most people are simply not foresighted enough to gather eyewitness vouchers at the time.

Viewed retroactively, the securing of affidavits for an action that occurred some years ago is beyond the scope of all but the most adroit *individual*. However, the procedure presents no insuperable problems when thought of in terms of the National Interest; which this certainly is, as noted in the Introduction. A nation can do anything it wants on its own soil, and sometimes on other people's.

But for the moment let us consider this stake-claiming as a purely domestic matter; time enough to go international arbitration, or worse, later on.

Take any country. Australia? It is near the start of the alphabet and a known paper air power. It was also very keen (if incomprehensible, as noted) in its recent efforts to get something gliding Down Under besides boomerangs. And it is *remote*—a significant factor, as we shall see.

The first thing Australia should have done, in our opinion, had they yearned to nail down the rights to the SST, score a solid scoop on the world, and garner a tidy little something gold-flow-wise, would have been the following:

1. Conduct a nation-wide search for the oldest man in Australia. Now this is not a mere piece of Sunday tabloidism like trying to ferret out the Loch Ness Monster or the Abominable Snowman. There is, without doubt, an Oldest Man in Australia. They would have found him somewhere, probably in a remote hamlet or sheep station. There seems to be a direct ratio between remoteness and longevity. Claimants to great age live neither anywhere close by, nor in a place that is at all stimulating. The cynical might opine that these far-flung locales are so dull that the inhabitants find diversion in lying to one another about their ages. It helps pass the time, which must get a little draggy after one has spent 100 years in Australia, or 160 years in the Caucasian People's Republic. (There is no paper in the Caucasus, therefore we may exclude their old-timers as claim-jumping possibles.)

2. When this oldest Australian had been located, the Governor-General or Prime Minister or some other top official (the higher the better, for the record) should have then taken a common, garden variety, delta wing, SST-prototype paper airplane and flashed it on him. And asked him The Questions: A) *Did you ever see one of these?* (Yes). B) *Did you ever make one?* (Sure). C) *When did you make the first one? What year?*

This last question is the pivotal one. Any answer before, let us say, 1847, properly notarized before the flower of Australian officialdom, would have certainly swung it for the Antipodes. Now, alas, it is too late.

This concludes the book proper. Now back to the Appendix.

Appendix I

LETTERS

A T THE OUTSET, we should note that hardly an entry was received at *Scientific American* that was not enclosed within, attached to, or otherwise associated with a letter. The first thing to be learned from this competition, it would seem, is that designers of paper airplanes are inveterate letter writers.

Some merely wished to express the importance of the event to them personally—Wanda Dillon of Hardy, Virginia, for example: "I would like to very much win because when I was making it [the plane] all the boys in my class laughed at me."

A great many entrants were frank to say that as they had never won anything at all before, they were hoping to win a Leonardo, at least.

Others merely wished to be friendly:

"My name is Jim Noble. My teacher is the greatest. Her name is Mrs. Jones. My mom's name is Maxine. My father's name is Vance and my brother's name (little) is David. I am in a class of 16 children here at Warren School. It is the best school. I am eleven years old and in the fifth grade. Very truly yours, Jim Noble, Terre Haute, Indiana."

By far the largest socio-economic group entering the competition were children, and by this we surmise that in terms of actual numbers young people tend to work with paper planes in greater quantity than older folk. Several of their entries are distinguished, we think, in design conception, as can be seen by Figures 10 through 13.

While we can credit children with the most intensive research, as the final advertisement pointed out, it was adults, and professional ones at that, who ultimately were victorious. Let's get on then, with the thinking of the adult mind.

Rev. M. Eugene Mockabee of the Lexington Theological Seminary in Lexington, Kentucky, tells us that he timed a paper plane's flight at three and one-half minutes, from a 400-foot railway bridge over the Kentucky River. Fuller Brush Man Waldridge Bailey counts among his better efforts a fifteen-minute flight from the thirty-sixth floor of 100 Park Avenue, "...utilizing a thermal rising from Pershing Square."

And from the New York Department of Housing and Urban Development, Mr. William Pain reports having launched "...a single delta from the 31st floor of the old Time-Life Building which soared for 1 hour and 33 minutes before disappearing *up and out of sight*." Mr. Pain notes that this took place during the "Golden Age of paper plane competition, before central air conditioning in high-rise office buildings."

San Francisco architect Felix Rosenthal is also a member of the Over-

One-Hour Club, having described a flight from Rockefeller Center, in which the plane ultimately disappeared over Times Square, somewhere. Mr. Rosenthal also tells us that he is the only known launcher of a paper plane across the Arno River; it was hurled from a second-story window.

Recalling his childhood in pre-depression Germany, Mr. Rosenthal enjoys remembering the days in grade school when the Jewish children were permitted a one-hour recess while their Christian classmates went to religious instruction. "That hour every week was just the time we needed to perfect our paper airplaning," so that

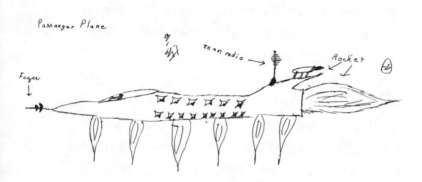

TIM SCHISLER, PORTLAND, OREGON

Fig. 10

Fig. 11

ROBYN REINEN, PORTLAND, OREGON

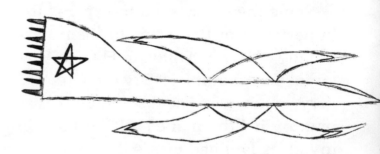

CLIFF SPECK, PORTLAND, OREGON

Fig. 12

Fig. 13

MARY SUE WUNDERLICH, PORTLAND, OREGON

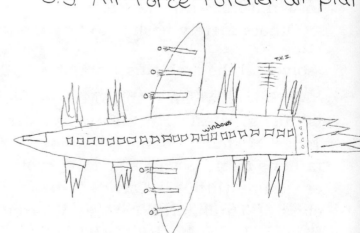

before long a clear superiority was established.

Mr. George S. Schairer, Vice President Research and Development, The Boeing Company, Seattle, Washington, writes of an early experience which might constitute an unofficial record for distance flown:

"During the summer of 1930, I was in Paris with a number of model airplane builders. We had been the winners of the American Boy model airplane contest, and during spare moments in Paris directed our attention to designing paper airplanes. One particular design proved to be very successful. I do not know who originated it, and certainly it was not me, but it is the best glider I have encountered among paper airplanes....We sailed possibly a thousand of these from the top of the Eiffel Tower, and picked one up at the Alexander III Bridge which is several miles away."

In another development, one reliable source has named a certain Mr. Yolen, who is President of the Kite Flyers Association of America, as having devised something known as the Ragallo Wing, which at once solves all the problems associated with the SST program. According to this source, Mr. Yolen's device, being an "evolved kite airfoil in concept, can be towed cross-country on long tether by *existing railroads*. No problems with the FAA...the developers of the Ragallo Wing need only have their lawyers remind FAA officials of 'rights-of-way' for railroads and there you have it. The passengers can ride down below in the train in maximum security and safety —enjoying the spectacle of the giant Ragallo Wing SST as it is towed across the land. And the problem of supersonic speeds is also surmounted, by placing the burden of its solution squarely where it belongs: on the railroads, not on the long-suffering aviation industry."

The spokesman for Mr. Yolen saw in this creation "the answer to the mass transport of millions." We could add that it has the apparent further advantage of a certain savings in development funds. And, too, there is the added pleasure of viewing the countryside and small towns as they go by, which will doubtless be found to be an exciting experience to travelers of the future.

Another San Francisco competitor, Mr. Frank Rosenberg, attached to his paper plane these thoughts on the future of air travel:

"The plane of the future will be a concept in reality transition rather than commutation. As house to airport commutation will be almost instantaneous, negative energies in relation to travel will be mitigated. Air travel will not appear unusual as air will be accepted as atmosphere similar to fish in water. As people travel more and more by air or underground, the earth's surface may be re-established for walking. The plane of the future will be more like a telephone experience than an exertion of physical energies. The plane will be a shuttle between realities and simplicity, and comfort will be more important than elegant meals, hostesses and in-flight movies."

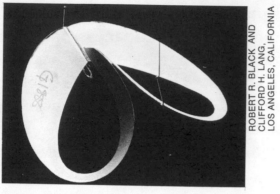

Fig. 14

We learn from Mssrs. Robert R. Black and Clifford H. Lang that their entry (Fig. 14) dates back in origin to Baron Von Lufthaven. The full story is an interesting one:

"Gentlemen:

The aircraft design herewith entered for competition is unique in that it has been handed down from father to illegitimate son for two centuries. Originally, the craft was designed and built by the legendary Baron Von Lufthaven, gentleman butcher, raconteur, and sportsman. Specifications for the craft's design and flight characteristics have been handed down through the family line by word of mouth only. This is the first public disclosure of the family secret.

"On April 1, 1767, the elder Luft-haven was preparing to draw and quarter a swine, the first step in preparing his then internationally famous specialty 'Luftwurst,' when one of his cuff protectors rolled off the chopping block and started to fall to earth. Suddenly, it attained stability and lift and glided past young Jukes, first illegitimate son of Lufthaven, who was cavorting on the ground on all fours, his normal position, having not yet learned to walk erect at the tender age of twenty-one. The sensitive young boy—ninth offspring of the gamekeeper's tender, mild and sympathetic daughter, Chatterley Dietrich—his scientific interest piqued, attempted to pick its wings off—his first inclination in the pursuit of knowledge. The boy's frustrated screams in finding that the object had no wings attracted his father's attention.

"Lufthaven, on discovering that the cuff protector actually flew, proceeded to expend the considerable family fortune over the remainder of his lifetime in developing the gliding-cuff concept into a profitable commercial venture, with no success. He eventually met his demise at the controls of a twelve-meter cuff launched from the signal tower of Lufthaven Schloss, thereby leaving a legacy of nothing but a gliding butcher's cuff in 18.66 generations of poor illegitimates."

Turning to more practical matters, the relationship between man-sized gliders and paper ones was explored by A. A. Backstrom of Dallas whose

[36]

A. A. BACKSTROM, DALLAS, TEXAS

Fig. 15   Backstrom's glider

paper glider was an outgrowth of a real one-man glider of his own design. A sturdy, handsome craft (see Fig. 15), Mr. Backstrom's glider inspired his paper entry which when tested in the competition finished about 5,000th.

As one further light on people's thoughts about the future of aeronautics, we refer to the drawing of Dennis

Fig. 16

DENNIS G. RIETZ, NORTH HIGHLANDS, CALIFORNIA

4t. INTERNATIONAL PAPER AIRPLANE COMPETITION

SUPERSONIC TRANSPORT
DESIGNED BY: *Dennis D. Rietz*   DATED 31 DEC, 1966
4824 WILLOW BROOK DR.
NORTH HIGHLANDS, CALIF.
EMPLOYER: US GOV'T CIVIL SERVICE,
NMER, MCCLELLAN AFB, CALIF.

OCCUPATION:
STATISTICAL
DRAFTSMAN

DESIGNER'S CONCEPTION
Scientific American,
Leonardo Trophy Competition,
415 MADISON AVE., NEW YORK
10017

NOTE:
WINGS FOLD
DOWN FOR
SLOW FLIGHT,
TAKE-OFF &
LANDINGS

TWO EA. PAPER AIRPLANE ENTRIES
ENCLOSED.
CLASS ENTERED: "ORIGAMI" FOR BOTH
(Leonardo Trophy Competition)   ENTRY'S
HOWEVER; BOTH ENTRIES
FLY.

Rietz, of North Highlands, California, shown in Figure 16. As can be seen, Mr. Rietz recommends that the wings of SST aircraft be designed to flap, as it were, depending upon whether one is in flight or slowing down for landings.

In another vein, we found this note both interesting and amusing:

拝礼

僕は英語が話せません。だから失礼ながら日本語で書かせていただきます。僕は6日の西日本新聞でこの事をしりました。興味がとてもわき出しいてもたっていもいられず。紙でこんな飛行機を作りました。僕はこのコンテストの規則を全くしりません。もししっかえなければこのコンテストにくわえて下さい。この飛行気の名前は「つばめ」と「みみ飛行機」と名づけました。「つばめ」をとばす時は はねおこすこしまるめてとは して下さい。お願いします。

日本
福岡市今川二丁目十三一西
三角福雄

サンエンティフィシク・アメリカン会社　様

And this one:

> Barclays Bank D.C.O.,
> Reef Trustee Branch,
> P.O. Box 8000,
> Johannesburg, South Africa

DEAR SIRS,

Enclosed is my entry to your competition.   (SIGNED) *D. L. Cairns*

I hereby certify that the above named is employed by Barclays Bank D.C.O.   (SIGNED) *L. Groom*

Before we get on with a few comments sent along by the winners to the competition, we want to reprint in its entirety a most involving report sent us by Mr. Joseph W. Dauben of Harvard University. We believe it will be self-explanatory.

2,

anonymous patrons of the sciences), whose airfoil presents certain unique advances, offers maximum surface area at a minimum cost (about $.02 per square inch).

It is clear from the Kutta–Joukowski theorem that $L = 2\pi k \rho V = 2\pi \rho V \int_{-c/2}^{c/2} k\, dx$

$= 2\rho V^2 \int_0^\pi (A_0 \tan \tfrac{1}{2}\theta + \sum_1^\infty A_n \sin n\theta) \tfrac{1}{2} c \sin\theta\, d\theta.$

assuming $n > 1$, we now have that
$\int_0^\pi \sin n\theta \sin\theta\, d\theta = 0$, and consequently
$L = c\rho V^2 \int_0^\pi (2A_0 \sin^2 \tfrac{1}{2}\theta + A_1 \sin^2\theta)\, d\theta = \pi c\rho V^2 (A_0 + \tfrac{1}{2}A_1)$. We can now show that the lift coefficient is
$C_L = \pi(2A_0 + A_1) = \pi(2\alpha + \tfrac{2}{\pi}\int_0^\pi \tfrac{dy}{dx}(1 + \cos\theta)\, d\theta) = 2\pi(\lambda_1 + \alpha)$ where
$\lambda_1 = \tfrac{1}{\pi}\int_0^\pi \tfrac{dy}{dx}(1 + \cos\theta)\, d\theta.$

It is now clear that $\lambda_1 + \alpha$ measures the absolute incidence; λ_1 gives us the direction of the axis of zero lift (see diagram following.)

---

(3)

Joseph W. Dauben
77 Perkins Hall
Harvard University
Cambridge, Massachusetts

G752

Saturday, January 14

Gentlemen,

Enclosed please find one paper airplane. Copies of the enclosed drawings and calculations have already been forwarded to Boeing and Lockeed in the hopes that they may profit from the important results of these researches.

You may find the following developments of interest. There has been considerable dispute over the theoretical lift coefficient and direction of the axis of zero lift we can expect when a paper airfoil of the kind described below is involved. The "Scientific American IV" (I, II and III, respectively, were realized only on paper; IV has become a realization only at the benevolence of certain

---

3.

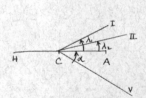

Since the airfoil AH in the paper model is flat, the center of the chord C is also the center of the profile (which is not always the case) so that the angle λ_1 determines I.

We now consider λ_1, integrating to obtain
$\tfrac{dy}{dx}(1 + \cos\theta) = \tfrac{2\,dy}{d\theta}\left(\tfrac{1 + \cos\theta}{\csc\theta}\right) = \tfrac{2}{c}\tfrac{dy}{d\theta}\cot\tfrac{1}{2}\theta$
hence
$\lambda_1 = \tfrac{2}{\pi c}\int_0^\pi \tfrac{dy}{d\theta}\cot\tfrac{1}{2}\theta\, d\theta =$
$\tfrac{2}{\pi c}\left(y\cot\tfrac{1}{2}\theta\right)\Big]_0^\pi + \tfrac{2}{\pi c}\int_0^\pi y\cdot\tfrac{1}{2}\csc^2\tfrac{\theta}{2}\, d\theta$

Now, at the leading edge, $\theta = \pi$, the integrated part vanishes; at the trailing edge the form is $0\cdot\infty$. It now follows that

4.

$$\lim_{\theta \to 0} y \cot \tfrac{1}{2}\theta = \lim_{\theta \to 0} \frac{y}{\sin \tfrac{1}{2}\theta} = \lim_{\theta \to 0} \frac{dy/d\theta}{d(\sin\tfrac{1}{2}\theta)/d\theta}$$

Applying l'Hospital's rule we can write

$$\frac{dy}{d\theta} = \frac{dy}{dx} \cdot \frac{dx}{d\theta} = \tfrac{1}{2} c \sin\theta \, \frac{dy}{dx}$$

It now follows that

$$\lim_{\theta \to 0} y \cot \tfrac{1}{2}\theta = \lim_{\theta \to 0} \left(\frac{dy}{dx} \, c \sin\tfrac{1}{2}\theta \right) =$$

0, unless $\frac{dy}{dx} \to \infty$ at the trailing edge. In the case of the paper airfoil, the profile coincide with the camber line and the difficulty is avoided.

We finally have that

$$\lambda_1 = \frac{2}{\pi} \int_0^\pi \frac{y}{c} \cdot \frac{1}{1-\cos\theta} \, d\theta .$$

The result can now be obtained graphically, and is left as an exercise.

Appreciating your concern in these matters. I remain,

Sincerely,
Joe Dauben

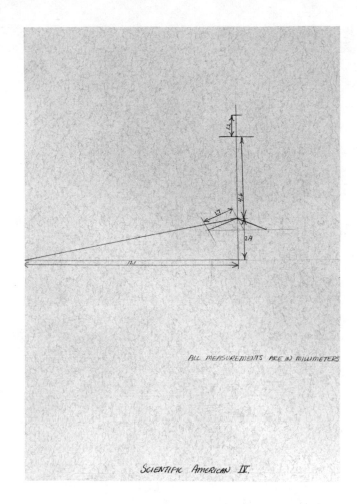

ALL MEASUREMENTS ARE IN MILLIMETERS

SCIENTIFIC AMERICAN IV.

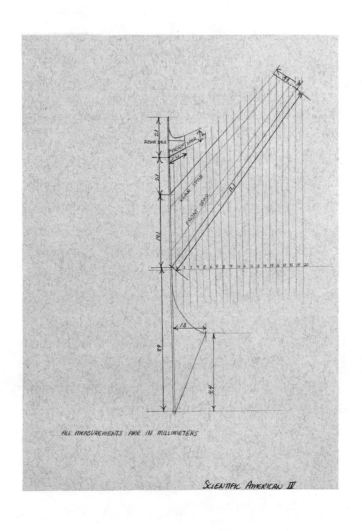

ALL MEASUREMENTS ARE IN MILLIMETERS

SCIENTIFIC AMERICAN IV

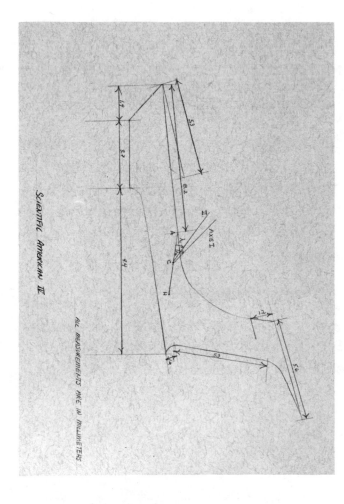

SCIENTIFIC AMERICAN IV

ALL MEASUREMENTS ARE IN MILLIMETERS

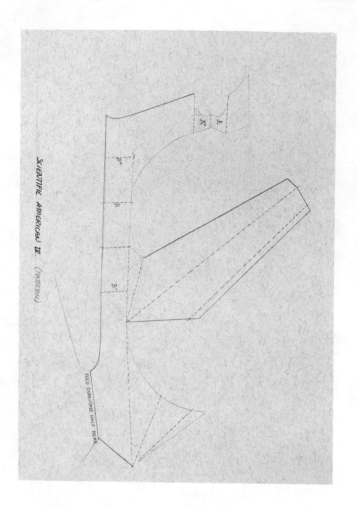

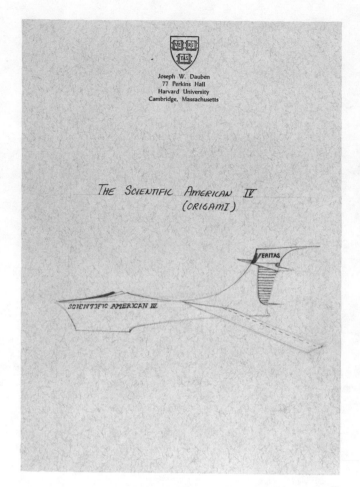

The third advertisement, announcing the winners of the competition, points out that all of them were in one way or another experienced in technical matters. Perhaps it should have been of little surprise to discover that men with some actual knowledge of what they were after, and with certain scientific data with which to work, achieved more than others.

Two of the seven winners knew Orville Wright personally. One of the winners, Captain Barnaby (see Fig. 17), is something of an air pioneer himself, being the first man to fly a sailplane launched from a dirigible, an achievement, among a long list of others, that has earned him the title Air Pioneer extended by the Air Association of the United States. As for Mr. Hooven, he went to some lengths in a letter describing his boyhood experiences with Mr. Wright (see p. 42).

Mr. Wright wasn't the only intimate of Mr. Hooven. In a letter to Fred Goerner, author of *The Search for Amelia Earhart,* Mr. Hooven reveals that just before Miss Earhart's departure on the ill-fated flight, "I installed one of the first prototypes of the modern aircraft radio direction-finder."

However, Mr. Hooven continues, "Before she embarked [it] was removed, and installed in its place was the old-fashioned null-type direction-finder that she carried with her. The modern instrument would have given her a heading on the transmitter of the cutter *Itasca* and on Howland Island even under poor reception conditions, and it would have shown her without ambiguity that her destination was still ahead."

Fig. 17   Captain Barnaby waves.

FREDERICK J. HOOVEN
910 SUNNINGDALE DRIVE
BLOOMFIELD HILL, MICHIGAN

January 26, 1967

Mr. Leonardo da Vinci
c/o SCIENTIFIC AMERICAN
Paper Airplanes Division
415 Madison Avenue
New York City, New York 10017

Dear Leonardo:

The enclosed folded paper flying wings are very little larger than the wing
section models Orville Wright and I tested nearly 50 years ago in his wind
tunnel. They have just a sufficient reflex trailing edge to keep center of
pressure travel within the stable range. If the duration and distance of
flight are measured in terms of steady state sinking rates and gliding angles
rather than in terms of how far somebody can throw the airplane, then these
models should perform pretty well. They are entered in those two categories.

In 1920, when I was a schoolboy of 15, four of my friends and I built an airplane. Orville Wright was one of the trustees of the school we went to, and
it seemed the natural thing to go to ask his advice about our plans and ideas.
He liked boys. I think he felt relaxed with them, and he didn't feel that
reservation that he felt with most adults who were trying to get him to endorse
something or to introduce somebody to somebody else, or one of those things
that people are always after a great man to do.

Anyway, however silent he was in public, and however reserved he was with
people he didn't know too well, he was kind and natural with us, and talked
for hours about aeronautics, the things he and Wilbur did, and the problems
they ran into and how they solved them.

Some people forget that boys can understand things, but he complimented us by
talking gravely and seriously just as he would have to any grown-up engineer.
Aeronautics had just gone through the impetus of the war of 1914-1918, and had
changed and developed rapidly. We read avidly all the textbooks and the publications of the National Advisory Committee for Aeronautics, which in those
days were written in terms that a 15-year-old could understand, and we could
soon see that so far as aeronautics was concerned, Orville had died when
Wilbur did. Nothing that he referred to or told us about in aeronautics dated
from a time after Wilbur's death, but what impressed us most was how much of
the whole problem of flight these brothers had thought about and dealt with
before that time.

We went back many times to the laboratory on Third Street. He was never too
busy to see us and talk about our problems. He didn't make us design the airplane as he would have done it. He would argue with us about fundamental
points about the wing sections and tell us how he and Wilbur found out how to
prevent spins, but he saved our pride. One of the things we argued about was
thick and thin wings. We wanted to use a thick wing and showed him the NACA
report that told how much better they were than the thin kind he wanted us
to use. He didn't get stuffy about this affront to his authority. He just
showed us the results of the tests that he and Wilbur had made in 1908 and
some in 1902. We found some of the old models and we made some of our own
and we tested them again in his wind tunnel, using the ingenious and elegant
little balance that he and Wilbur had used to measure the tiny forces on
the model airfoils. The results were just as he told us they would be. We
decided to use a thin wing.

It had happened to him before and he had learned to believe his and Wilbur's
experiments, even when they made liars out of some eminent authority like the
NACA or Simon Newcom (who had proved that flight was impossible), or Samuel
Langley. We believed them too.

Years later we learned about Reynolds numbers and the affect of air viscosity on small-scale low-speed results. Modern aerodynamics has forgotten what might be called the third range, or the viscous sub-subsonic range of aerodynamics, but it played an important part in the early development of the airplane.

The Wright Brothers wind tunnel used airfoils having a span of six inches and a chord of one inch at an air speed of about 40 miles per hour or 59 feet per second. All of the early wind tunnels were of comparable dimensions and air speed. Of these probably the outstanding was that of Eiffel (the builder of the Eiffel Tower).

When the velocities and dimensions are both small, the effects of air viscosity produce a more laminar and less turbulent flow, and since the effects of viscosity and scale effects were not then recognized, the designs of early full-scale aircraft embodied the erroneous conclusions of the small scale wind tunnels of the day. One of the most important of these errors was to indicate the superiority of thin wing sections, which showed much better ratios of drag to lift than any thick wing. This explains the early prevalence of biplanes or monoplanes with many brace wires. Tony Fokker, who was only 19 at the time and too young to know better, was the first to use an internally braced thick wing on a full-sized airplane.

However erroneous the early wind tunnel results were as they applied to full-scale aircraft, they still apply to model airplanes and particularly to folding-paper airplanes. It is only a coincidence that the thin wing is better than the thick wing for supersonic aircraft. The folding-paper airplane is still best understood in terms of pre-1915 aerodynamics.

Sincerely,

ORIGINAL SIGNED BY

Frederick J. Hooven

FJH/lee

The origami winner, Dr. Sakoda (see Fig. 18), who is also an expert in computer programming, reports,

"...there appear to be some common skills required in computer programming and origami...and I have come across a number of programmers who are also paperfolders. One common requirement is the fitting of parts into a circumscribed area . . . i.e., to work spatially in a restricted environment."

Dr. Sakoda then points out that "...because of the need to conserve space in an aircraft, the art of paper folding may be of use to someone, say, going to the moon."

And on that thought we close.

Fig. 18   Dr. Sakoda shown here among other favorite origami creations.

Fig. 19

JOHN CRAIG AND GEORGE PECK,
NEW YORK, NEW YORK

Fig. 20   Pocket Rocket. Instructions:
Wrap aluminum foil around upper half
of paper match. Push straight pin up
under foil to head of match and remove
again, leaving an exhaust channel. Place
match on opened paper clip and hold
lighted match to tip. Step back.

S. J. TWEEDIE AND F. D. WOODRUFF,
FALLS CHURCH, VIRGINIA

Fig. 21

Y. HIHOMIYA,
TOKYO, JAPAN

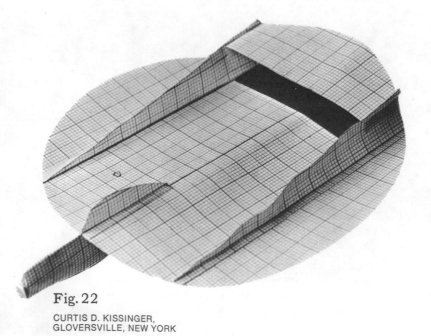

Fig. 22

CURTIS D. KISSINGER,
GLOVERSVILLE, NEW YORK

Fig. 23

LOUIS W. SCHULTZ,
OAK BROOK, ILLINOIS

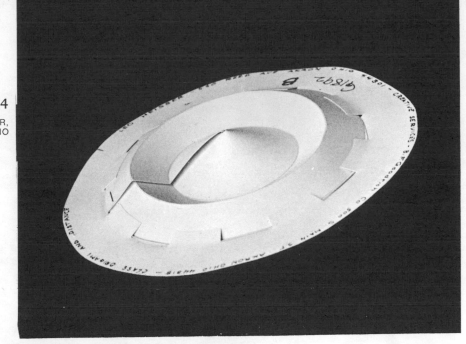

Fig. 24

LEO HEISSER,
AKRON, OHIO

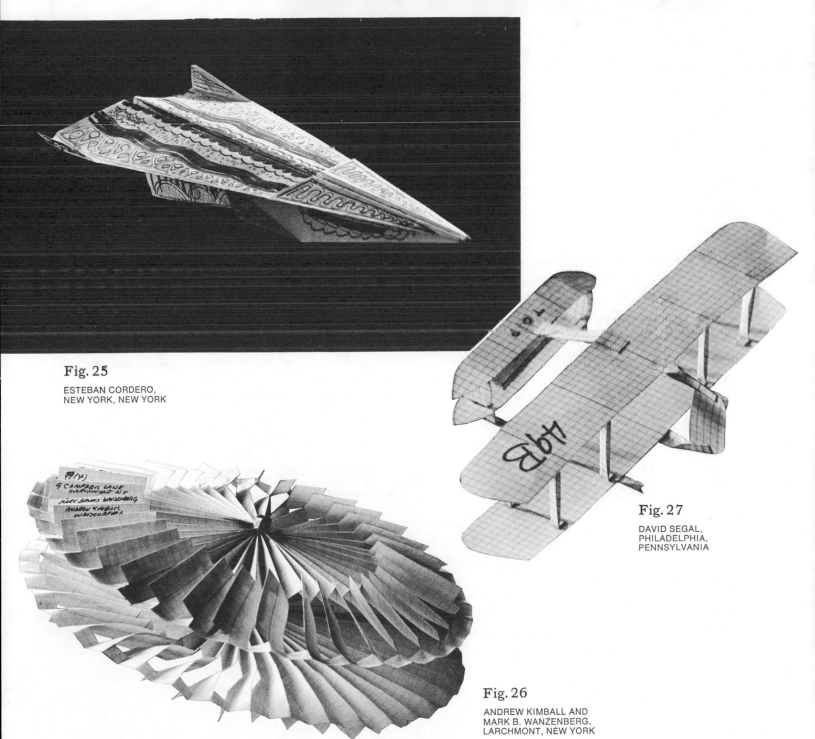

Fig. 25

ESTEBAN CORDERO,
NEW YORK, NEW YORK

Fig. 27

DAVID SEGAL,
PHILADELPHIA,
PENNSYLVANIA

Fig. 26

ANDREW KIMBALL AND
MARK B. WANZENBERG,
LARCHMONT, NEW YORK

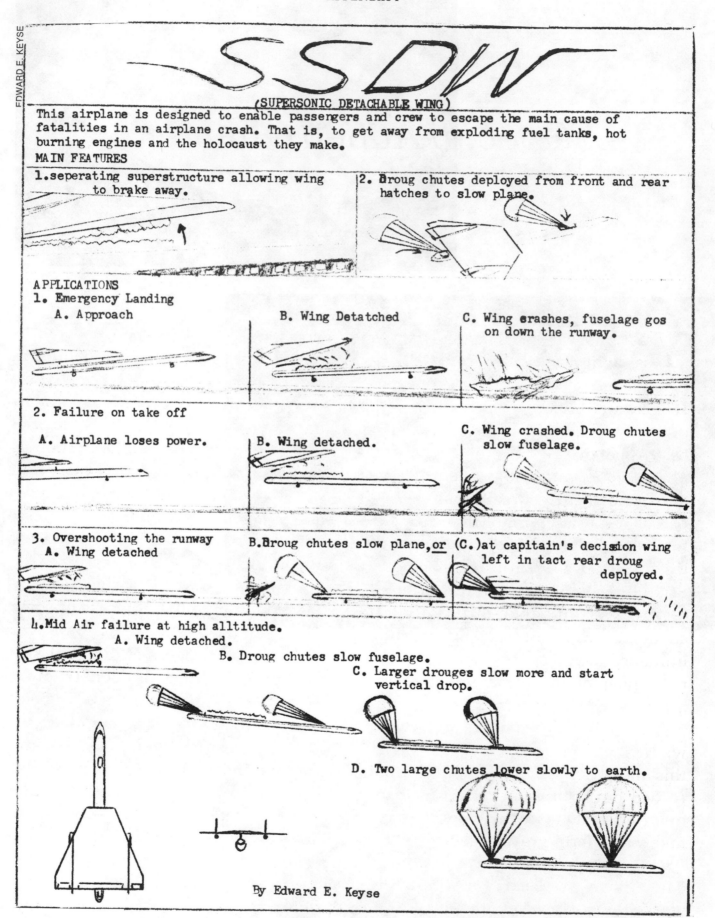

SSDW

(SUPERSONIC DETACHABLE WING)

This airplane is designed to enable passengers and crew to escape the main cause of fatalities in an airplane crash. That is, to get away from exploding fuel tanks, hot burning engines and the holocaust they make.

MAIN FEATURES

1. seperating superstructure allowing wing to brake away.

2. Droug chutes deployed from front and rear hatches to slow plane.

APPLICATIONS

1. Emergency Landing
   A. Approach
   B. Wing Detatched
   C. Wing erashes, fuselage gos on down the runway.

2. Failure on take off
   A. Airplane loses power.
   B. Wing detached.
   C. Wing crashed. Droug chutes slow fuselage.

3. Overshooting the runway
   A. Wing detached
   B. Droug chutes slow plane, or (C.) at capitain's decision wing left in tact rear droug deployed.

4. Mid Air failure at high alltitude.
   A. Wing detached.
   B. Droug chutes slow fuselage.
   C. Larger drouges slow more and start vertical drop.
   D. Two large chutes lower slowly to earth.

By Edward E. Keyse

Fig. 28   Keyse's Supersonic Detachable Wing

Special Added Chapter

A FLY IT YOURSELF COMPENDIUM

YOU MAY WONDER what a Chapter is doing back here after the Appendix and where exactly Appendix II is located. Fact is, the authors had every intention of having *this* section be "Appendix II," but our publisher pointed out that these twenty tear-out, fold-them-yourself paper airplanes constituted more than half the total volume of the book and ought at least be given the status of "Chapter." Still, though, as one of the primary features of any tear-out is that it should be torn out without creating immense havoc to the binding of the remainder of the book, which is required to stay in place, there was simply no moving this chapter up forward where the other one is. We tell you all this merely to assure you that what turned out to be a peculiar arrangement of sections in this book has not taken that form gratuitously.

One more word about the drawings. They have all been very carefully worked out. However, the success of each plane depends upon how faithfully you attend to minor details in folding and cutting and how patiently you experiment with various launching efforts. (Some models will do well with brisk arm tosses; others, such as Captain Barnaby's winning entry and Mr. Hooven's, require very gentle release from upheld hands.)

The pattern pages are perforated, as you see, so as to more easily allow you to tear them out and fold. Despite this, you may find in the case of some planes that your success improves with your own paper of different size and weight. Serious constructors might do well to purchase a bond paper pad from an art supply store. They come in different sizes and weights and fold nicely. It may also be helpful to try a prototype airplane on bond paper before attempting to build the plane from the printed page itself—practice, in paper airplanes as in all things, makes perfect!

THE AUTHORS

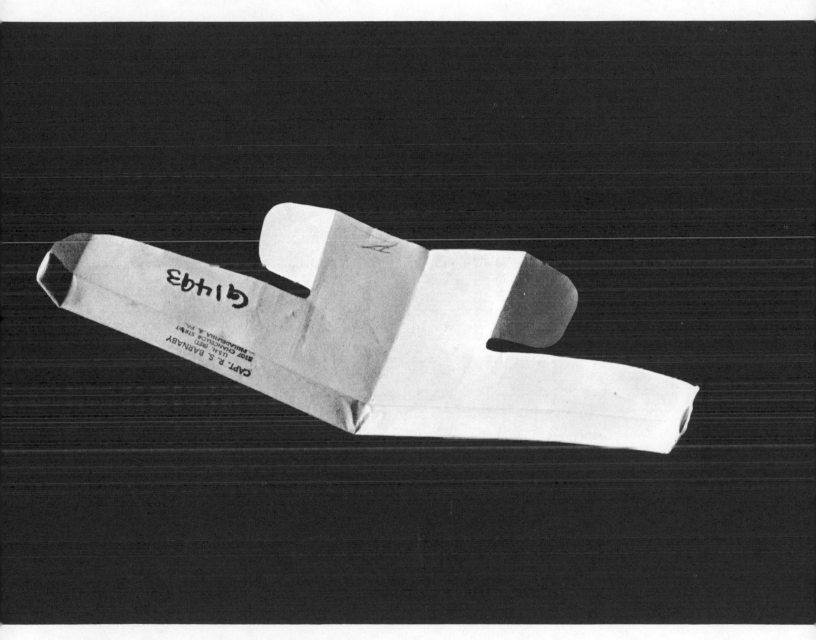

*WINNER: AEROBATICS/PROFESSIONAL
Capt. R. S. Barnaby U.S.N. (Ret.)
Philadelphia, Pa.
*(Exhibits consultant, The Franklin Institute; pioneer
aviator with title of "Elder Statesman of Aviation")*

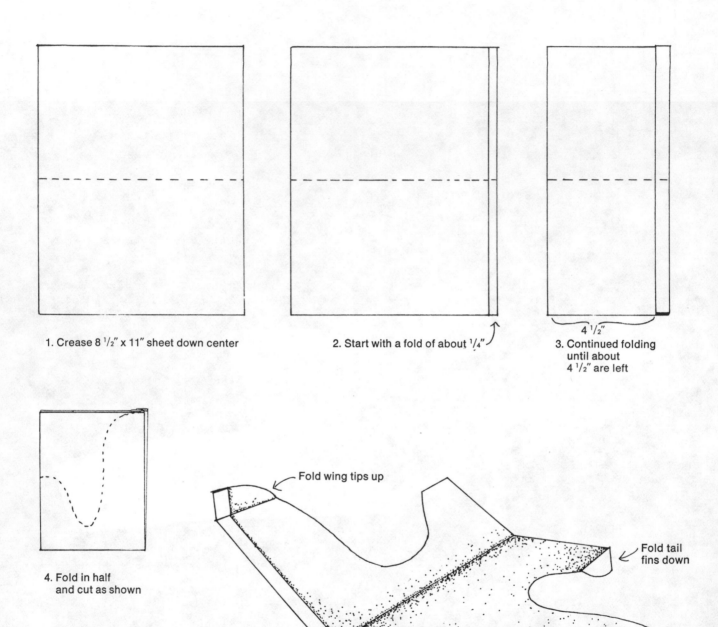

1. Crease 8 ½″ x 11″ sheet down center

2. Start with a fold of about ¼″

3. Continued folding until about 4 ½″ are left

4 ½″

4. Fold in half and cut as shown

Fold wing tips up

Fold tail fins down

Bend up

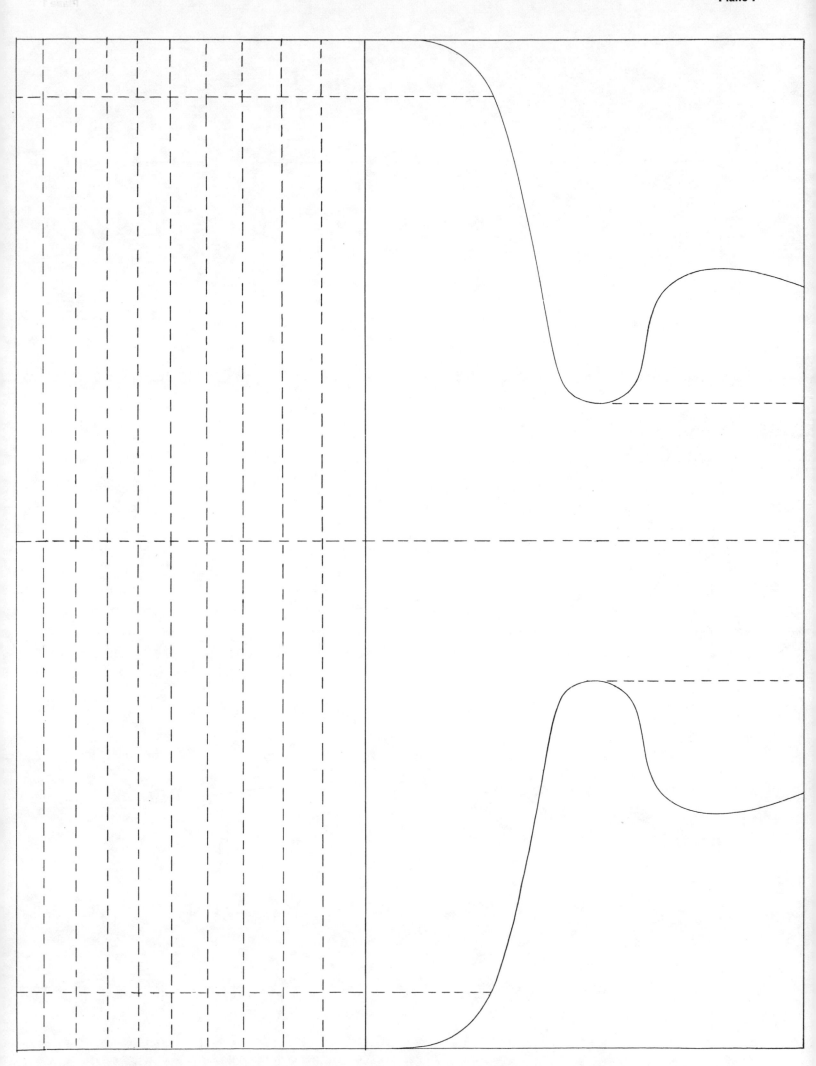

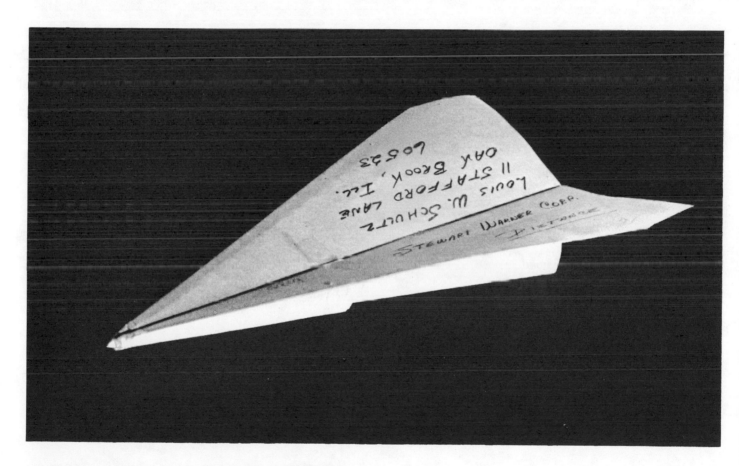

*WINNER: DISTANCE FLOWN/PROFESSIONAL
Louis W. Schultz
Oak Brook, Illinois
(Employed at Stewart Warner Corp.)

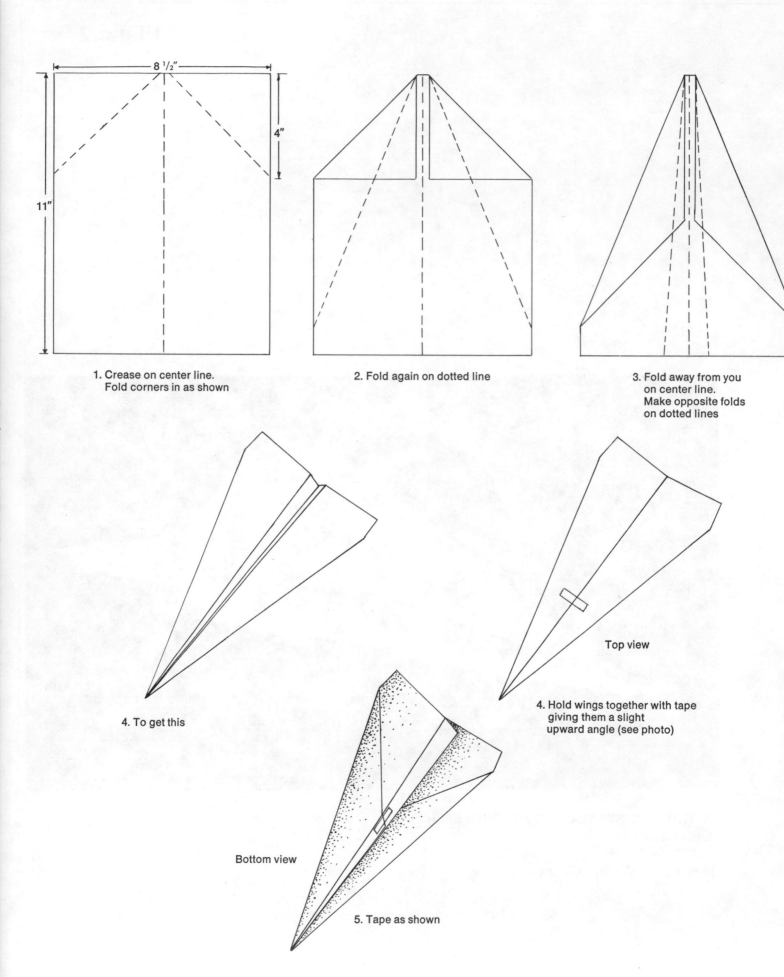

8 1/2"

4"

11"

1. Crease on center line.
   Fold corners in as shown

2. Fold again on dotted line

3. Fold away from you
   on center line.
   Make opposite folds
   on dotted lines

4. To get this

Top view

4. Hold wings together with tape
   giving them a slight
   upward angle (see photo)

Bottom view

5. Tape as shown

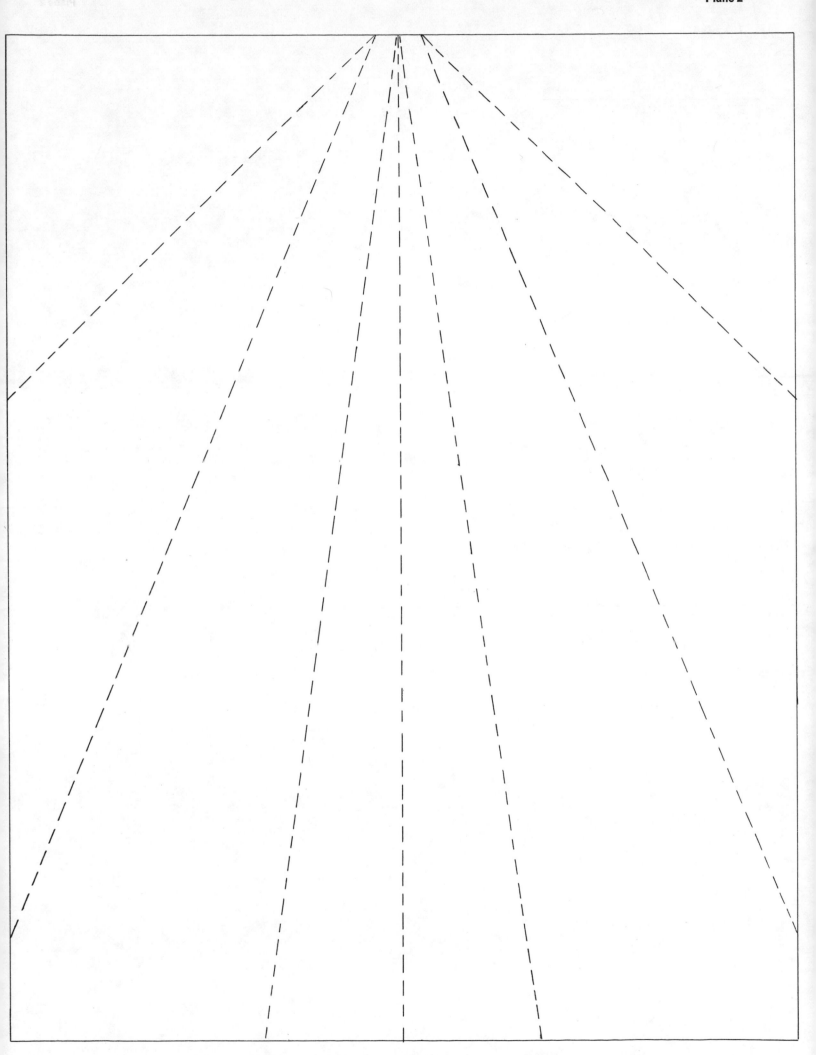

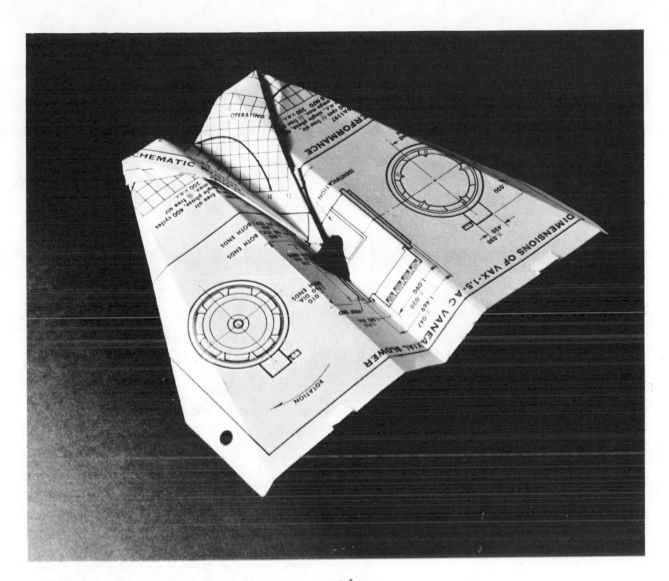

*WINNER: DURATION ALOFT/NONPROFESSIONAL
Jerry A. Brinkman
Dayton, Ohio
(*Assistant sales manager, Globe Industries*)

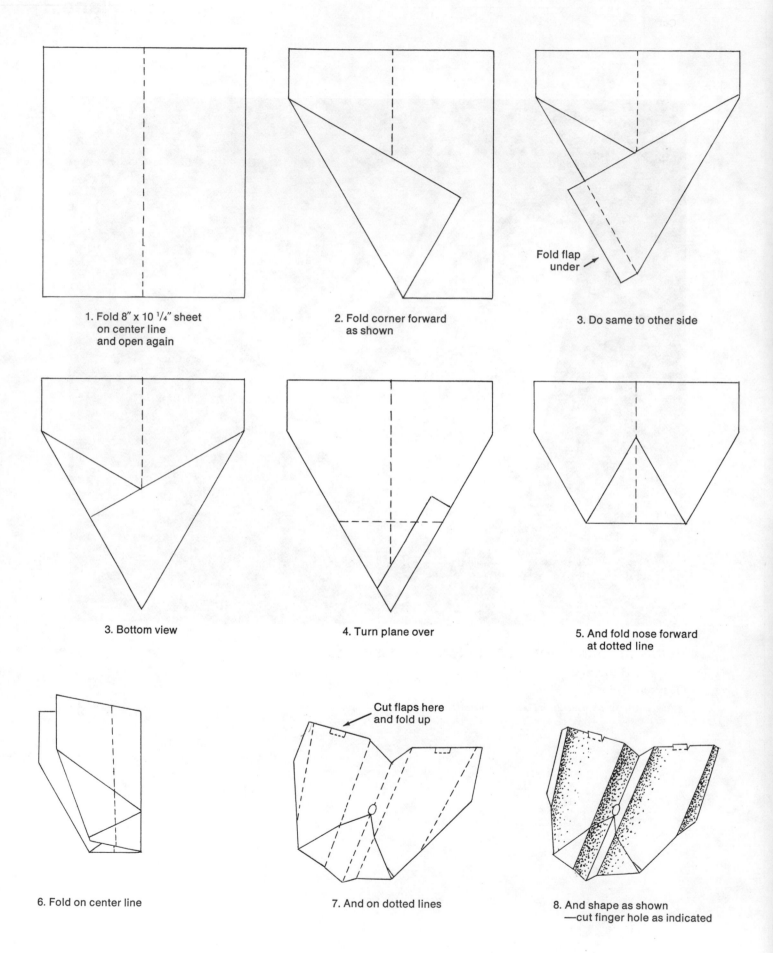

1. Fold 8″ x 10 ¼″ sheet
   on center line
   and open again

2. Fold corner forward
   as shown

3. Do same to other side

Fold flap
under

3. Bottom view

4. Turn plane over

5. And fold nose forward
   at dotted line

6. Fold on center line

Cut flaps here
and fold up

7. And on dotted lines

8. And shape as shown
   —cut finger hole as indicated

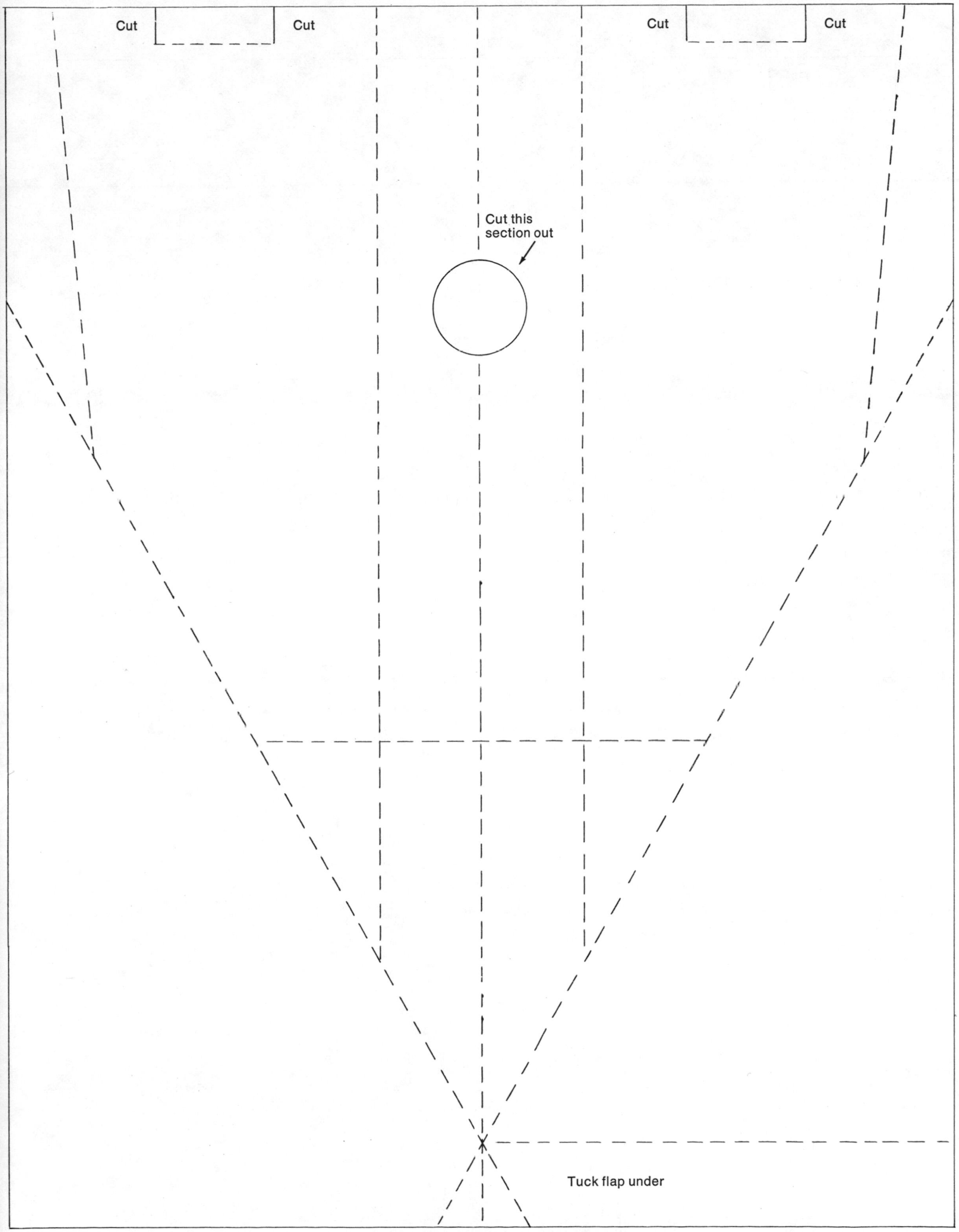

Cut

Cut

Cut

Cut

Cut this
section out

Tuck flap under

*WINNER: DURATION ALOFT/PROFESSIONAL
Frederick J. Hooven
Bloomfield Hills, Michigan
*(Subscriber and special consultant to
general manager, Ford Div., Ford Motor Co.)*

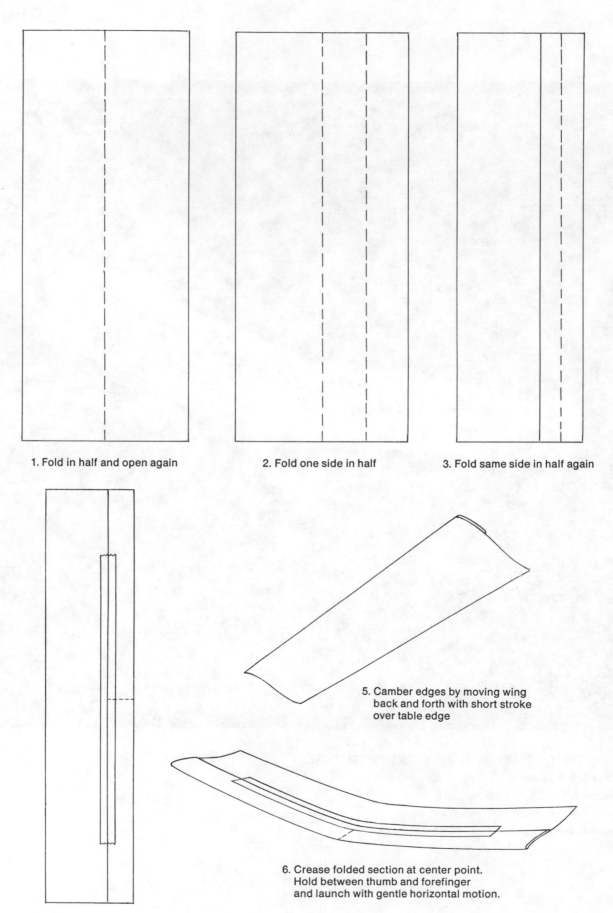

1. Fold in half and open again

2. Fold one side in half

3. Fold same side in half again

4. Fold over again; Tape

5. Camber edges by moving wing back and forth with short stroke over table edge

6. Crease folded section at center point. Hold between thumb and forefinger and launch with gentle horizontal motion.

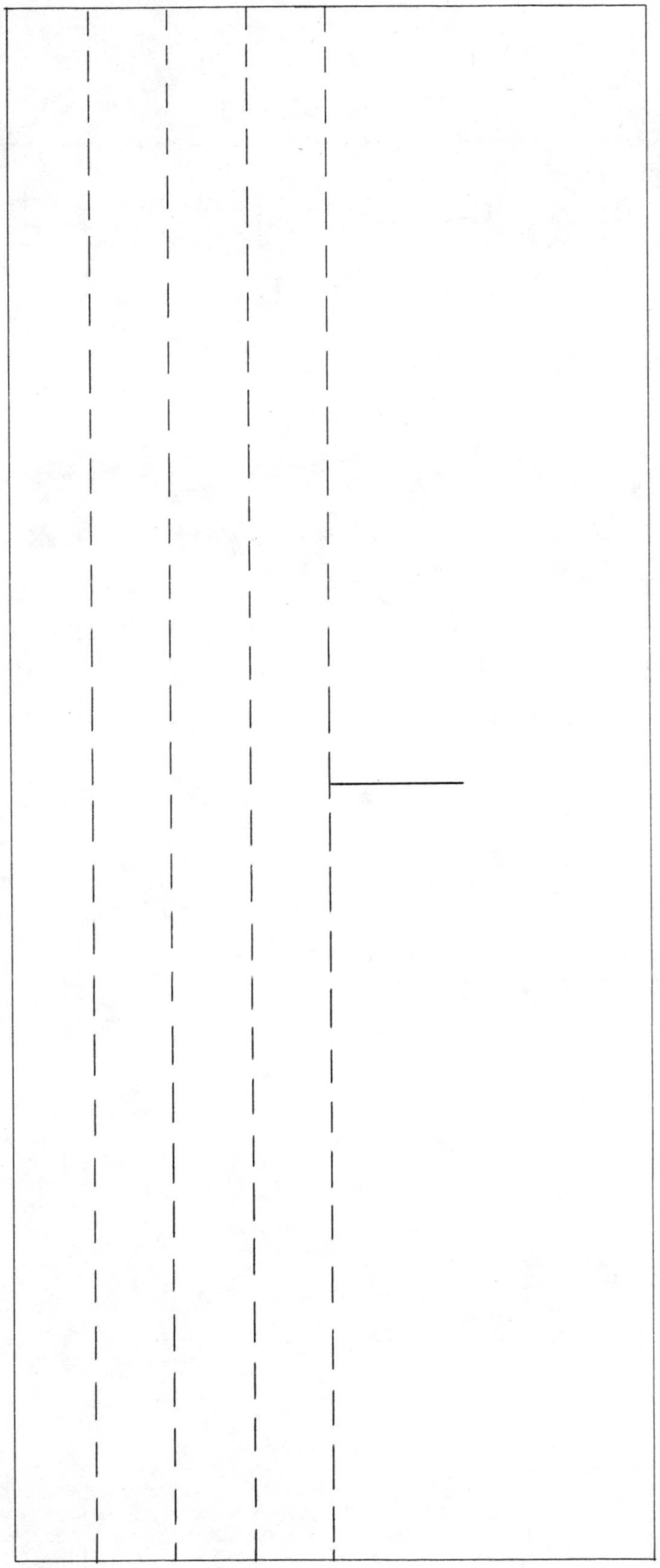

*WINNER: AEROBATICS/NONPROFESSIONAL
Edward L. Ralston
Urbana, Illinois
(Employed at Clark, Dietz & Associates)

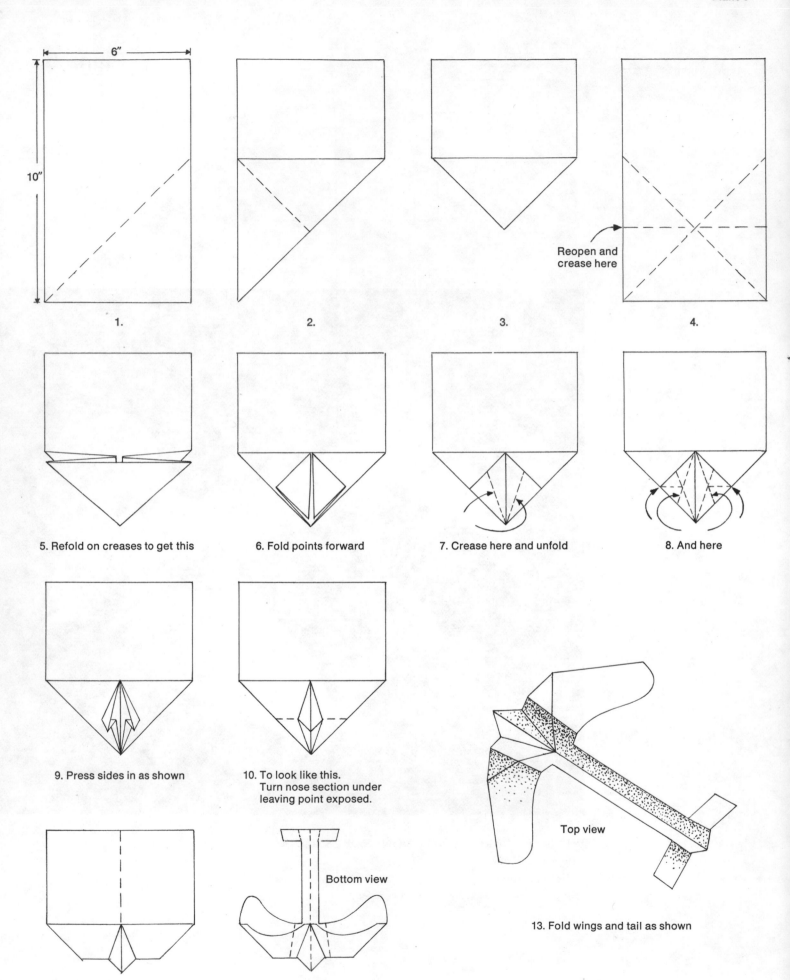

6"

10"

1.

2.

3.

4.

Reopen and crease here

5. Refold on creases to get this

6. Fold points forward

7. Crease here and unfold

8. And here

9. Press sides in as shown

10. To look like this.
Turn nose section under
leaving point exposed.

Top view

11. Fold in half on center line.
Trim out plane shape
(see pattern)

12. Trim out part
of under wing
to reduce weight

Bottom view

13. Fold wings and tail as shown

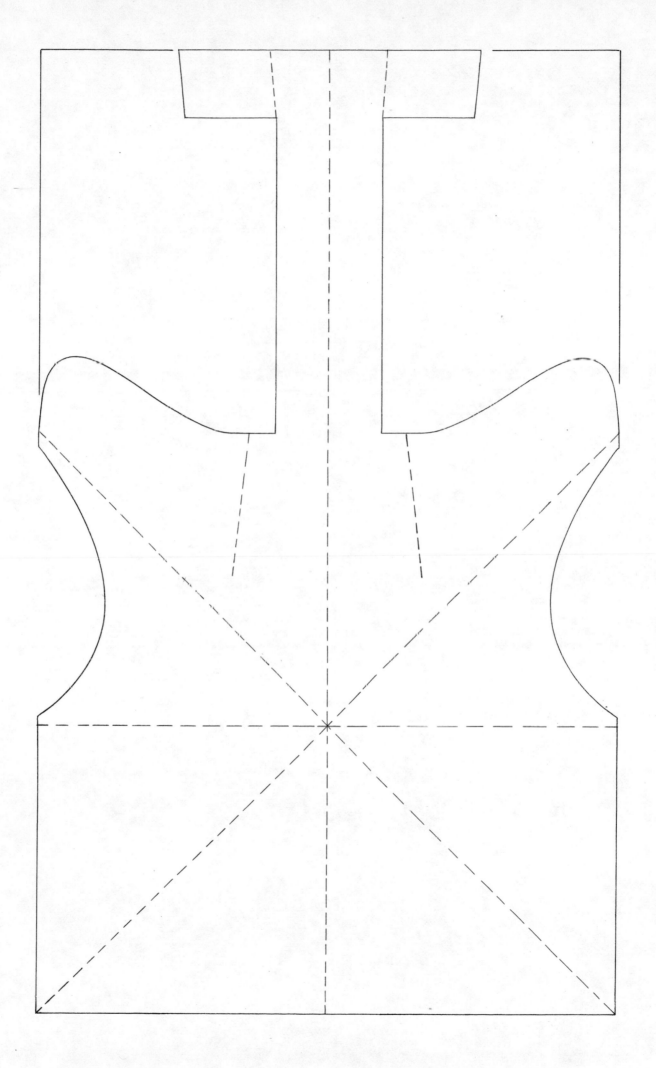

*WINNER: DISTANCE FLOWN/NONPROFESSIONAL
Robert B. Meuser
Oakland, California
*(Physicist, Lawrence Radiation Laboratory,
University of California at Berkeley)*

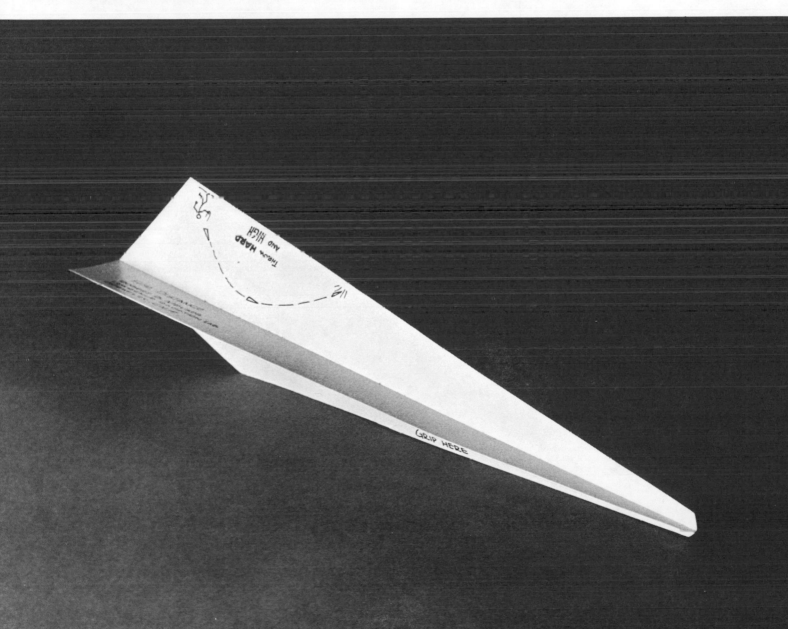

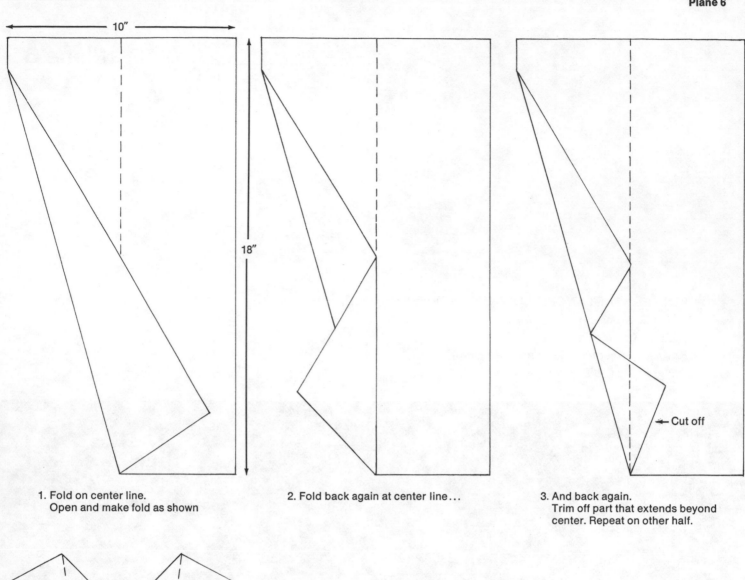

10"

18"

← Cut off

1. Fold on center line.
   Open and make fold as shown

2. Fold back again at center line…

3. And back again.
   Trim off part that extends beyond
   center. Repeat on other half.

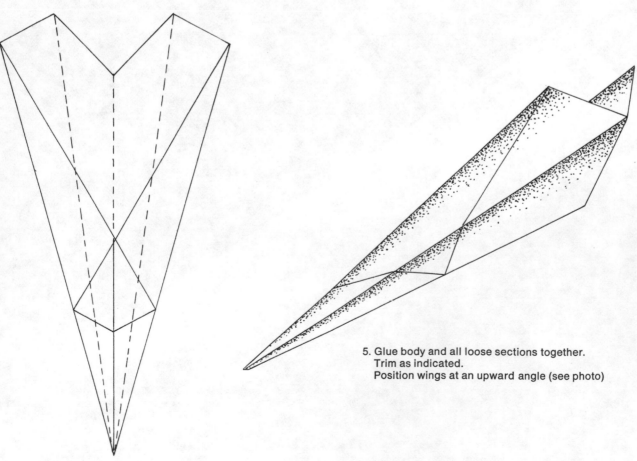

4. Fold down on center line.
   And up on sides

5. Glue body and all loose sections together.
   Trim as indicated.
   Position wings at an upward angle (see photo)

Note: Winning entry was made with heavy art paper 10" x 18"

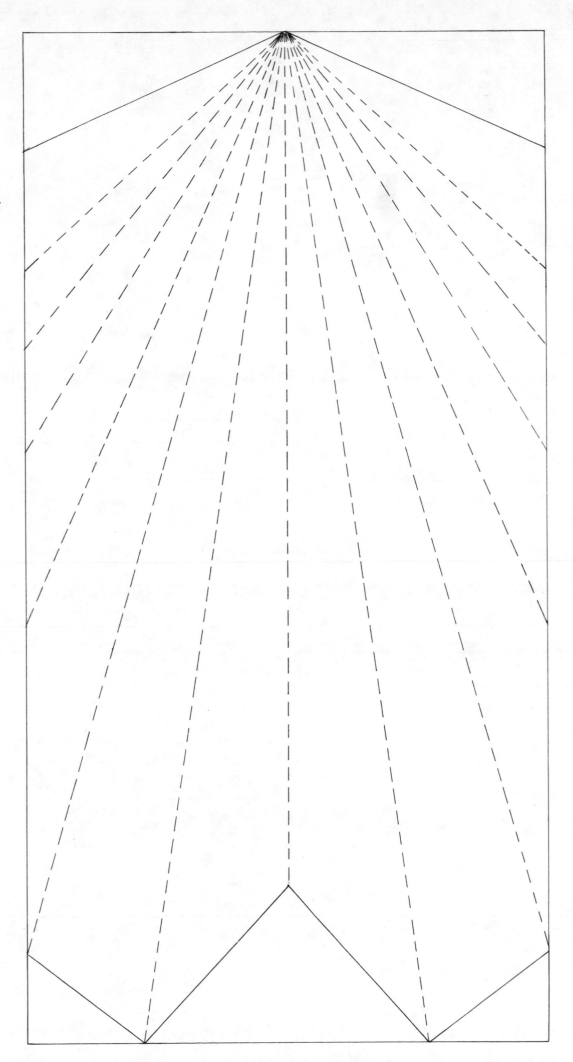

Winning plane
was made
with heavy paper
10″ x 18″

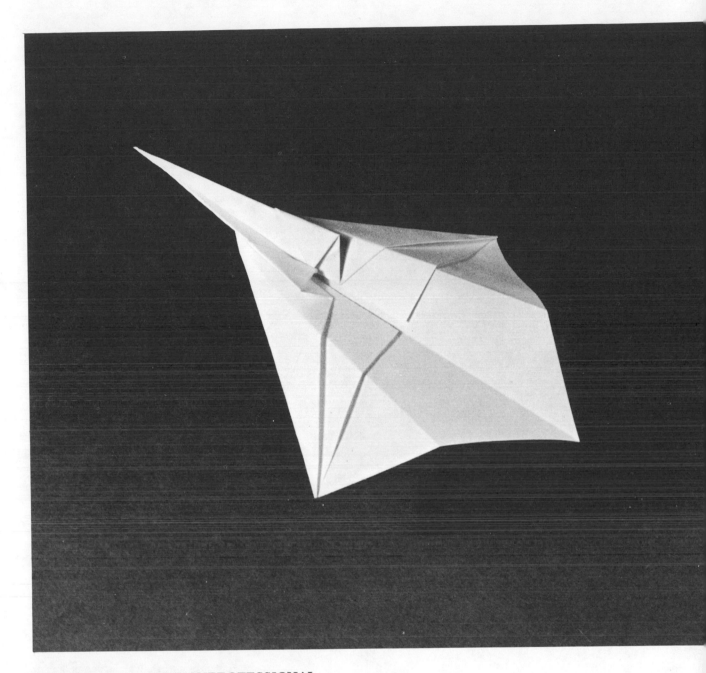

*WINNER: ORIGAMI/NONPROFESSIONAL
Professor James M. Sakoda
Department of Sociology and Anthropology
Brown University
Providence, Rhode Island

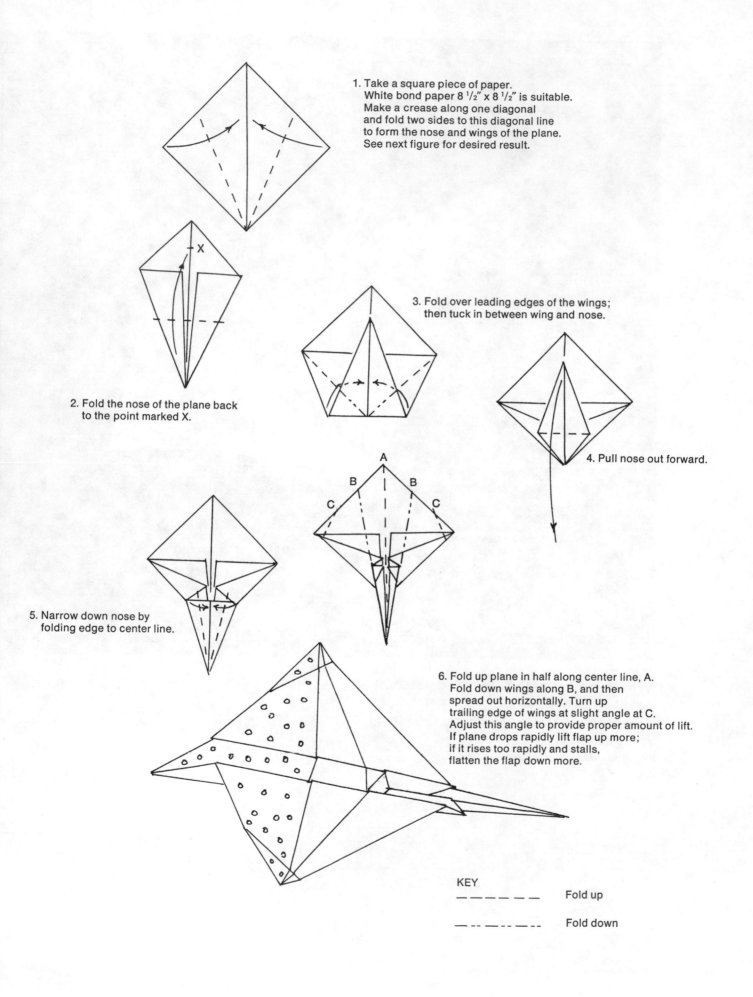

1. Take a square piece of paper.
   White bond paper 8 ¹/₂″ x 8 ¹/₂″ is suitable.
   Make a crease along one diagonal
   and fold two sides to this diagonal line
   to form the nose and wings of the plane.
   See next figure for desired result.

X

2. Fold the nose of the plane back
   to the point marked X.

3. Fold over leading edges of the wings;
   then tuck in between wing and nose.

4. Pull nose out forward.

A

B   B

C   C

5. Narrow down nose by
   folding edge to center line.

6. Fold up plane in half along center line, A.
   Fold down wings along B, and then
   spread out horizontally. Turn up
   trailing edge of wings at slight angle at C.
   Adjust this angle to provide proper amount of lift.
   If plane drops rapidly lift flap up more;
   if it rises too rapidly and stalls,
   flatten the flap down more.

KEY

— — — — — —   Fold up

— · · — — · · — ·   Fold down

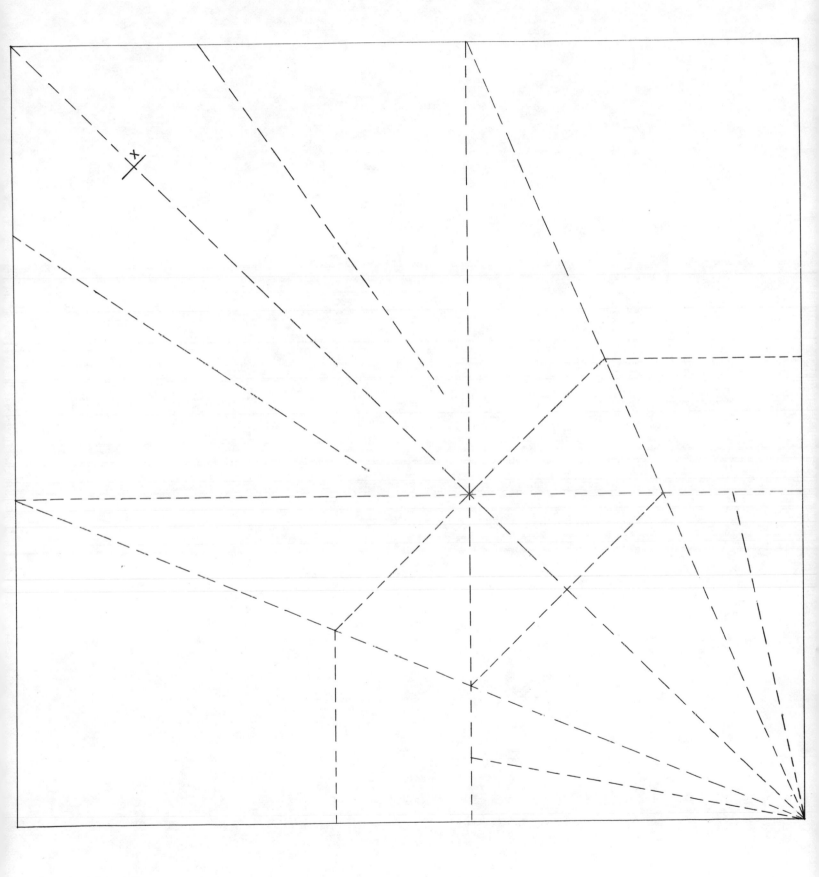

*WINNER: WESTERN DIVISION
Lewis G. Lowe
San Francisco, California
(Artist with Walter Landor & Associates)

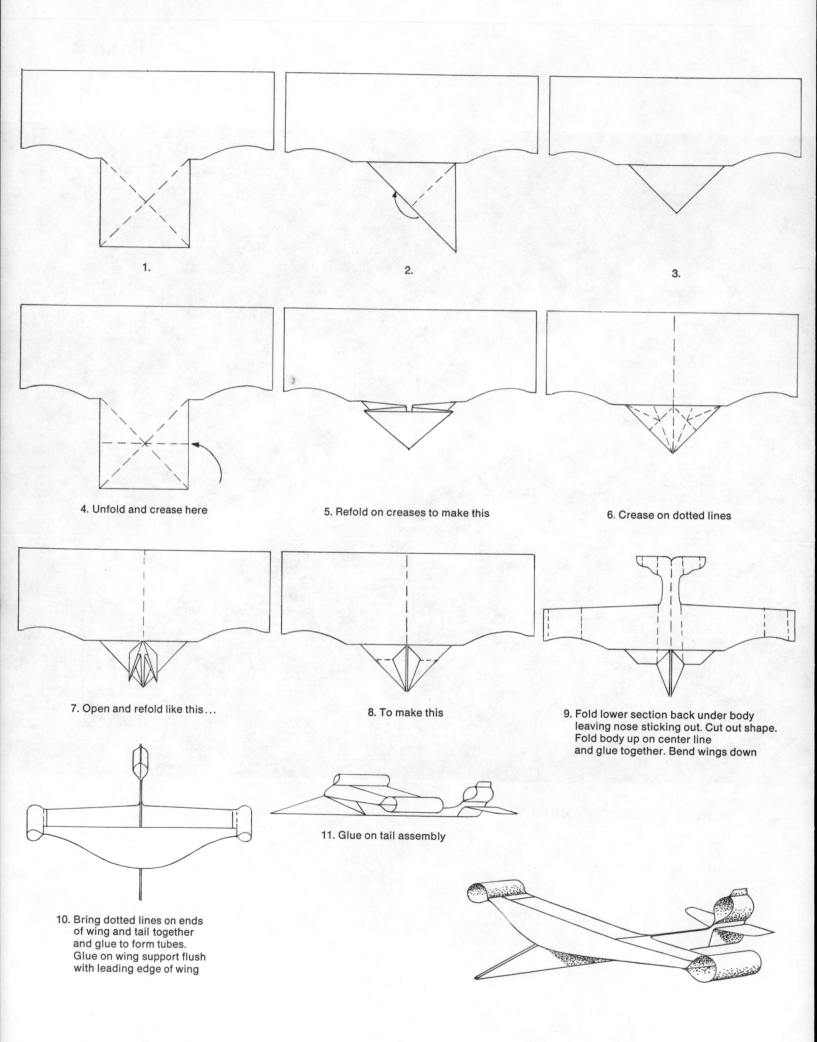

1.

2.

3.

4. Unfold and crease here

5. Refold on creases to make this

6. Crease on dotted lines

7. Open and refold like this...

8. To make this

9. Fold lower section back under body leaving nose sticking out. Cut out shape. Fold body up on center line and glue together. Bend wings down

11. Glue on tail assembly

10. Bring dotted lines on ends of wing and tail together and glue to form tubes. Glue on wing support flush with leading edge of wing

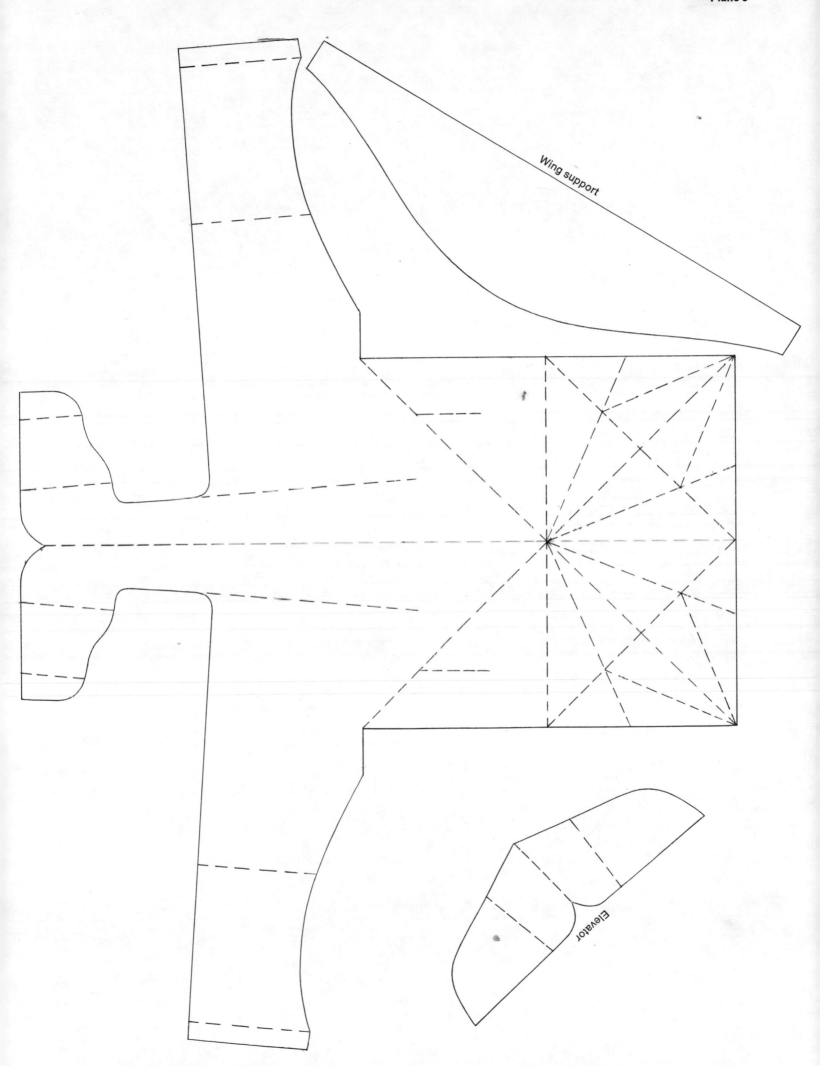

Wing support

Elevator

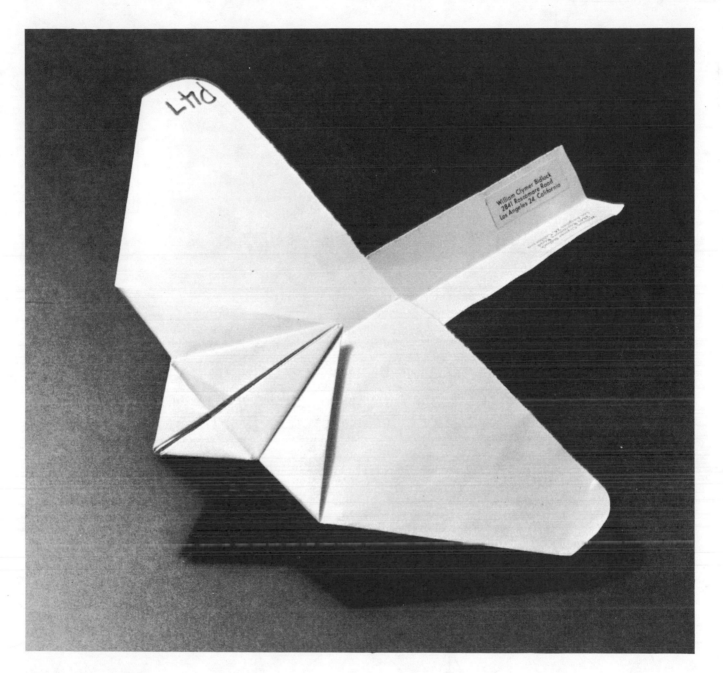

William Clymer Bidlack
Los Angeles, California
(Customer relations, Lockheed Aircraft)

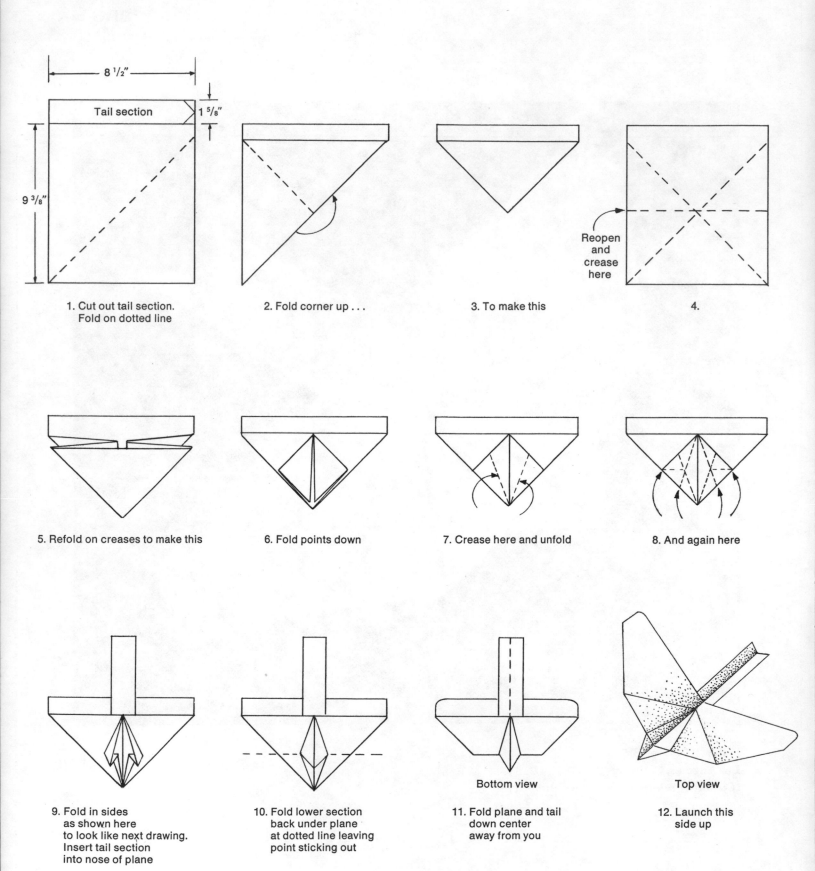

8 ½"

Tail section 1 ⁵/₈"

9 ³/₈"

1. Cut out tail section.
   Fold on dotted line

2. Fold corner up . . .

3. To make this

Reopen and crease here

4.

5. Refold on creases to make this

6. Fold points down

7. Crease here and unfold

8. And again here

9. Fold in sides
   as shown here
   to look like next drawing.
   Insert tail section
   into nose of plane

10. Fold lower section
    back under plane
    at dotted line leaving
    point sticking out

Bottom view

11. Fold plane and tail
    down center
    away from you

Top view

12. Launch this
    side up

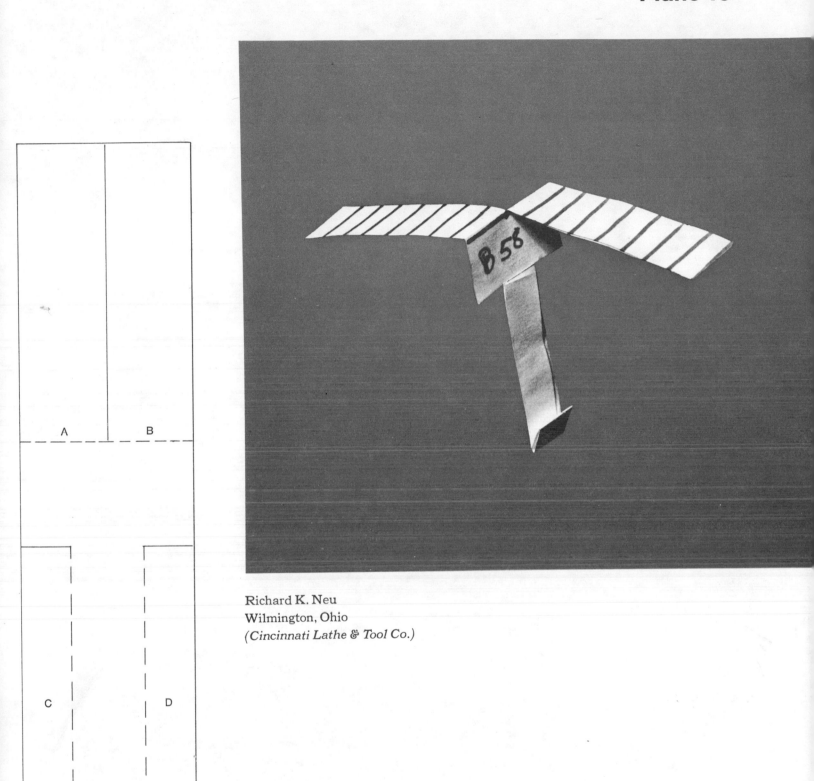

Richard K. Neu
Wilmington, Ohio
(Cincinnati Lathe & Tool Co.)

← INSTRUCTIONS

Cut along all solid lines.
Fold A forward. Fold B backward.
Fold C in and overlap by folding D.
After folding C and D fold up at E.
Launch by dropping from high position

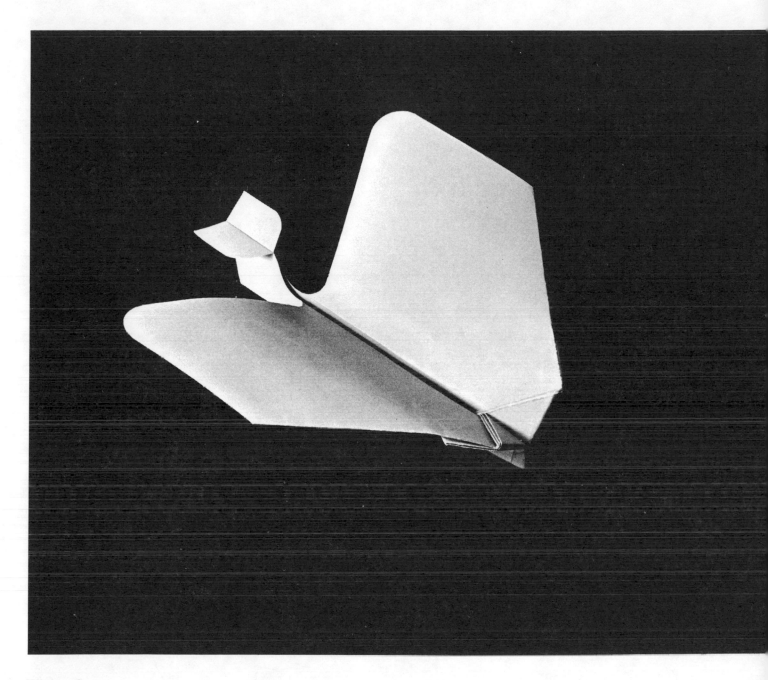

William Seno
Hackensack, New Jersey
(*Employed at Raymond Loewy/Wm. Snaith*)

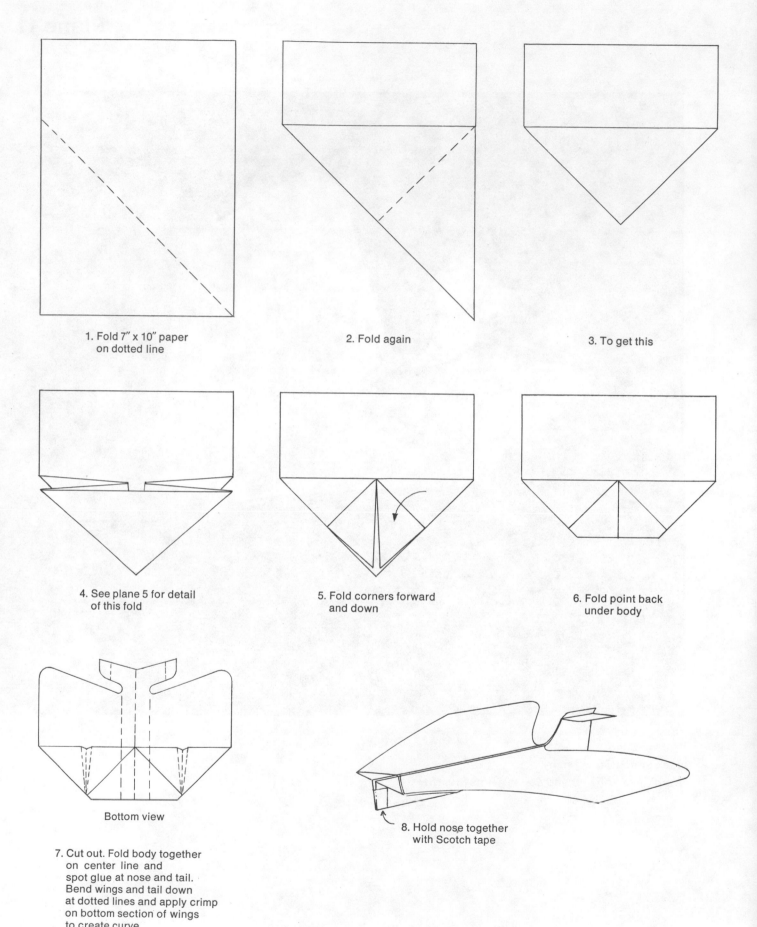

1. Fold 7" x 10" paper
   on dotted line

2. Fold again

3. To get this

4. See plane 5 for detail
   of this fold

5. Fold corners forward
   and down

6. Fold point back
   under body

Bottom view

7. Cut out. Fold body together
   on center line and
   spot glue at nose and tail.
   Bend wings and tail down
   at dotted lines and apply crimp
   on bottom section of wings
   to create curve

8. Hold nose together
   with Scotch tape

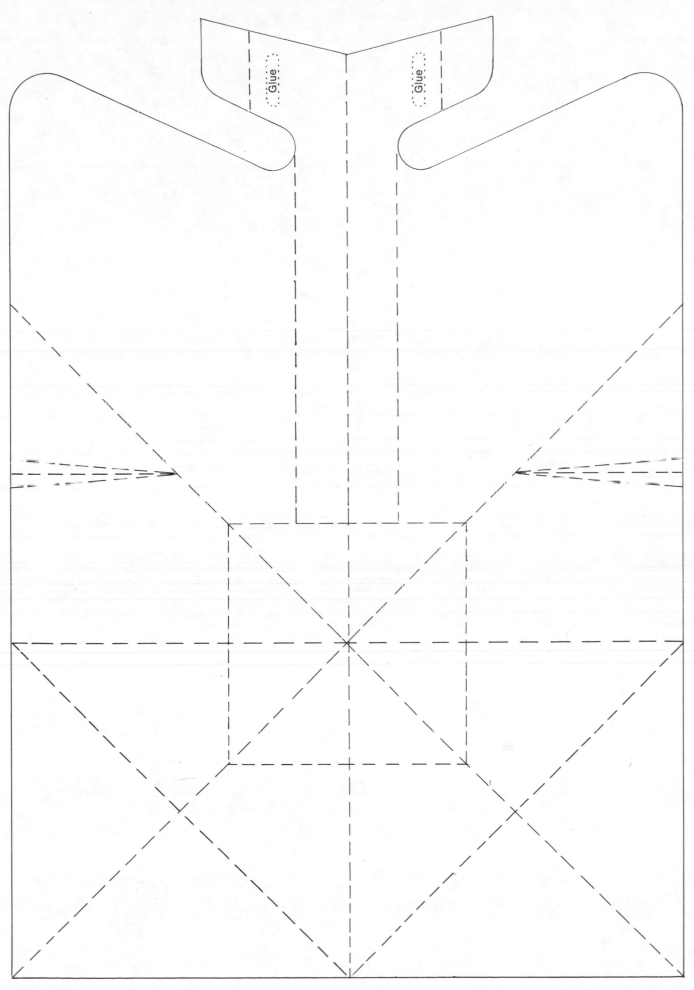

Glue

Glue

Start folding with lines on back

Plane 12

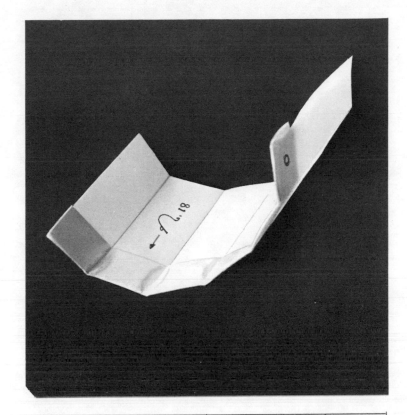

Nori Sinoto
New York City

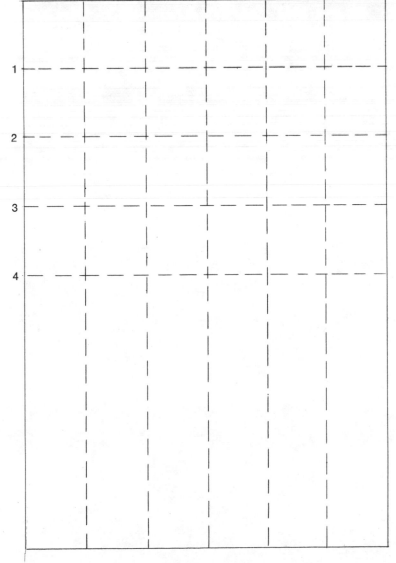

Fold at 2. Then 1 and 3 together.
Fold again at 4. After fold is
in position, crease along
vertical bottom lines
to form a gentle curve

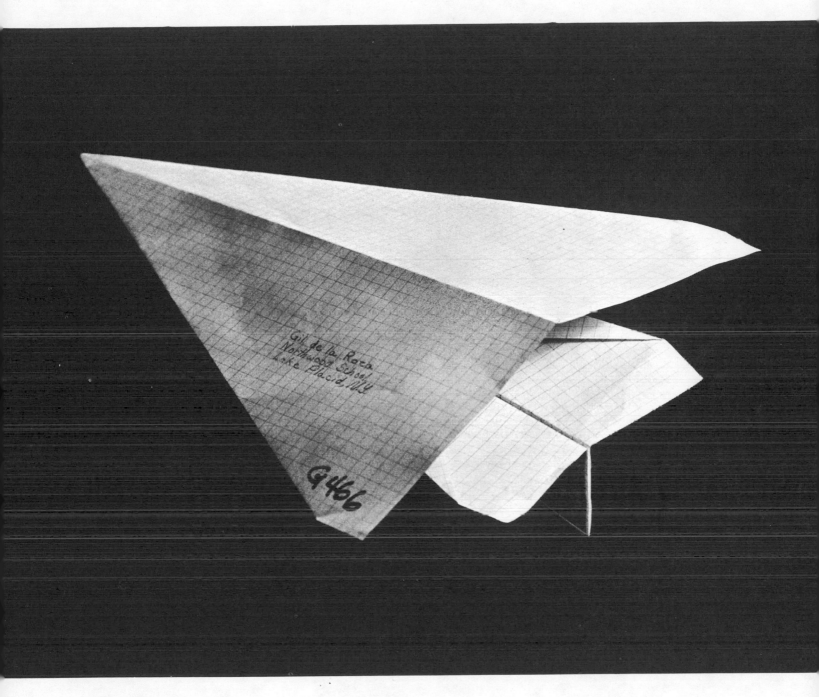

Gil de la Roza
Northwood School
Lake Placid, New York

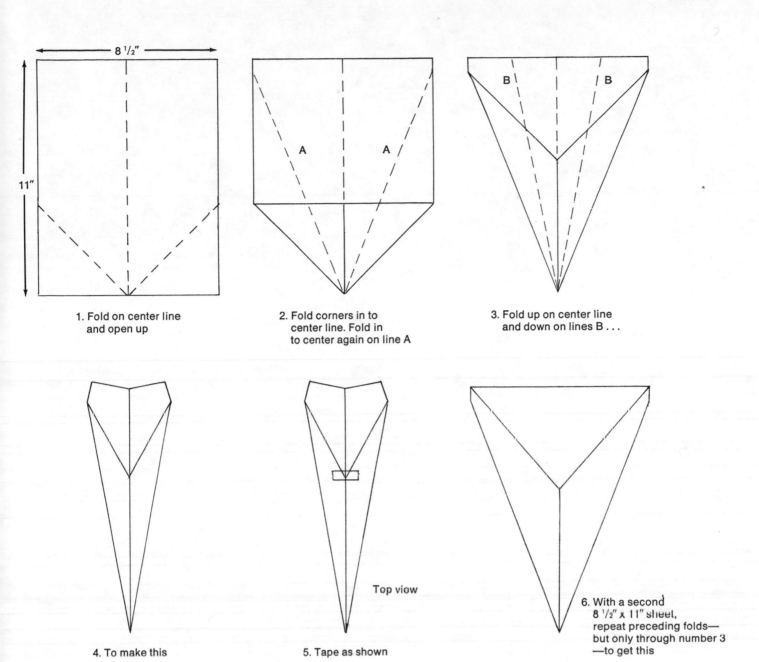

8 ½"

11"

1. Fold on center line
   and open up

2. Fold corners in to
   center line. Fold in
   to center again on line A

A   A

3. Fold up on center line
   and down on lines B . . .

B   B

4. To make this

5. Tape as shown

Top view

6. With a second
   8 ½" x 11" sheet,
   repeat preceding folds—
   but only through number 3
   —to get this

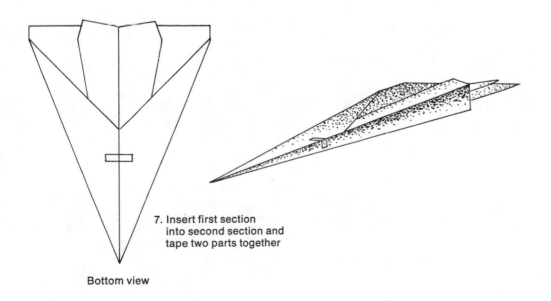

7. Insert first section
   into second section and
   tape two parts together

Bottom view

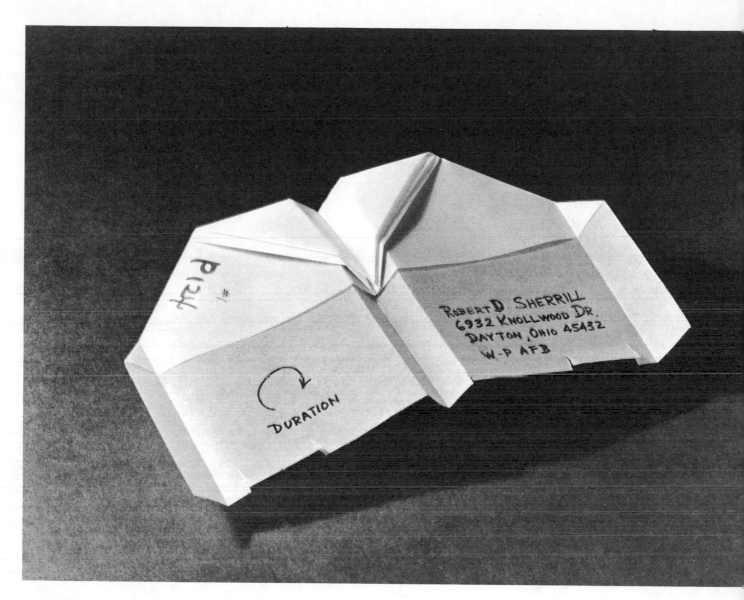

Robert D. Sherrill
Dayton, Ohio
(Employed at Wright-Patterson AFB)

Original entry was made of tracing paper

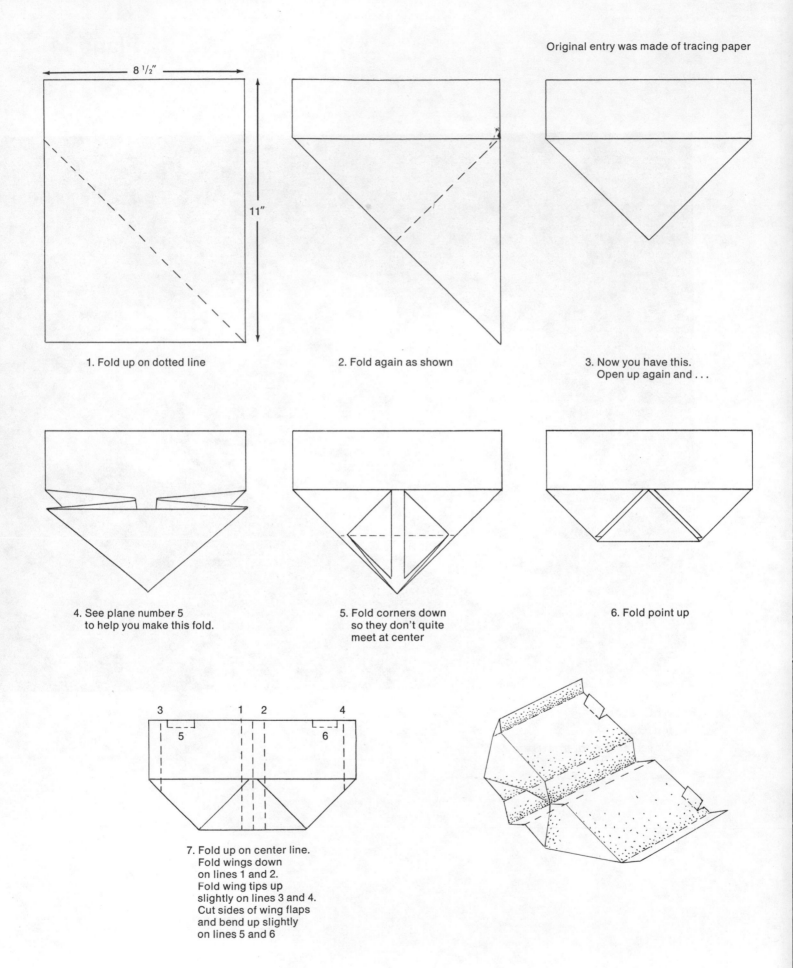

8 ½"

11"

1. Fold up on dotted line

2. Fold again as shown

3. Now you have this.
   Open up again and . . .

4. See plane number 5
   to help you make this fold.

5. Fold corners down
   so they don't quite
   meet at center

6. Fold point up

3   1 2   4
5   6

7. Fold up on center line.
   Fold wings down
   on lines 1 and 2.
   Fold wing tips up
   slightly on lines 3 and 4.
   Cut sides of wing flaps
   and bend up slightly
   on lines 5 and 6

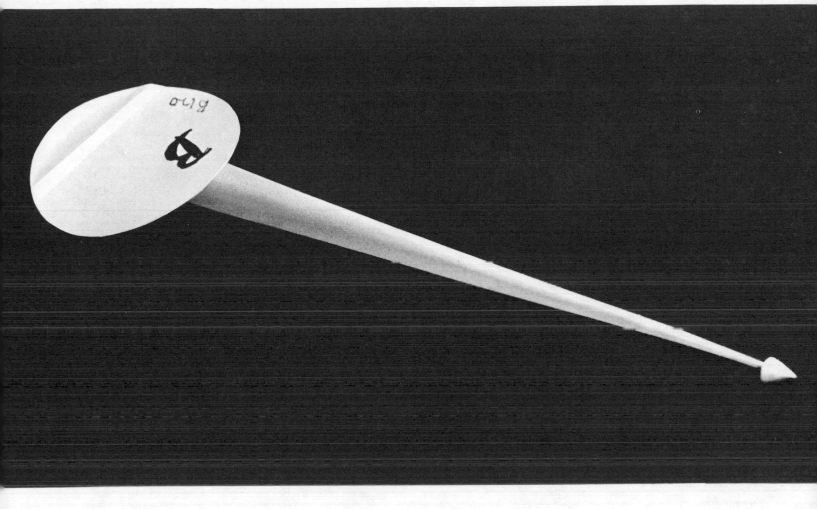

Yvon Belisle
Montreal, Canada
(*Employed at Telemetropole Corp.*)

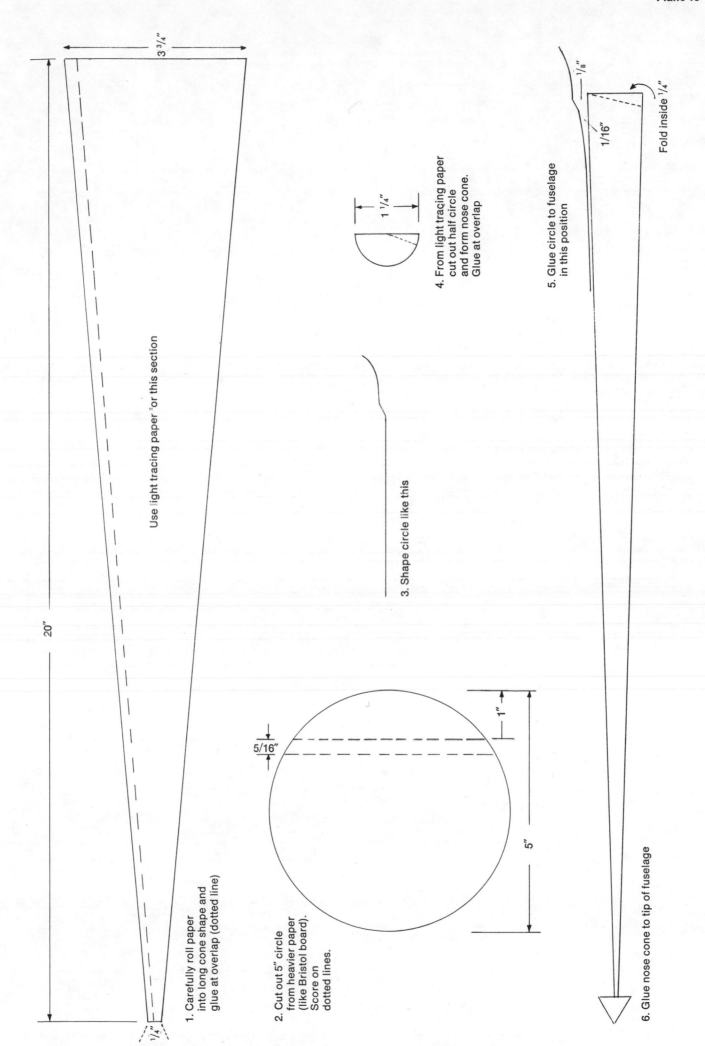

3 ³/₄"

20"

Use light tracing paper for this section

1. Carefully roll paper into long cone shape and glue at overlap (dotted line)

¹/₄"

2. Cut out 5" circle from heavier paper (like Bristol board). Score on dotted lines.

5/16"

1"

5"

1 ¹/₄"

4. From light tracing paper cut out half circle and form nose cone. Glue at overlap

3. Shape circle like this

¹/₈"

1/16"

Fold inside ¹/₄"

5. Glue circle to fuselage in this position

6. Glue nose cone to tip of fuselage

Chuck Casell
New York
(Doyle Dane Bernbach, Media Dept.)

INSTRUCTIONS →

Fold at center line. Unfold and fold at 1.
Hold down and fold at 2. Fold at center
and then fold away from center at 3 to
form wing. Fold up at 4 to form
stabilizer. After folding is completed,
cut along solid lines 5—double up on dotted line
to lock body together.

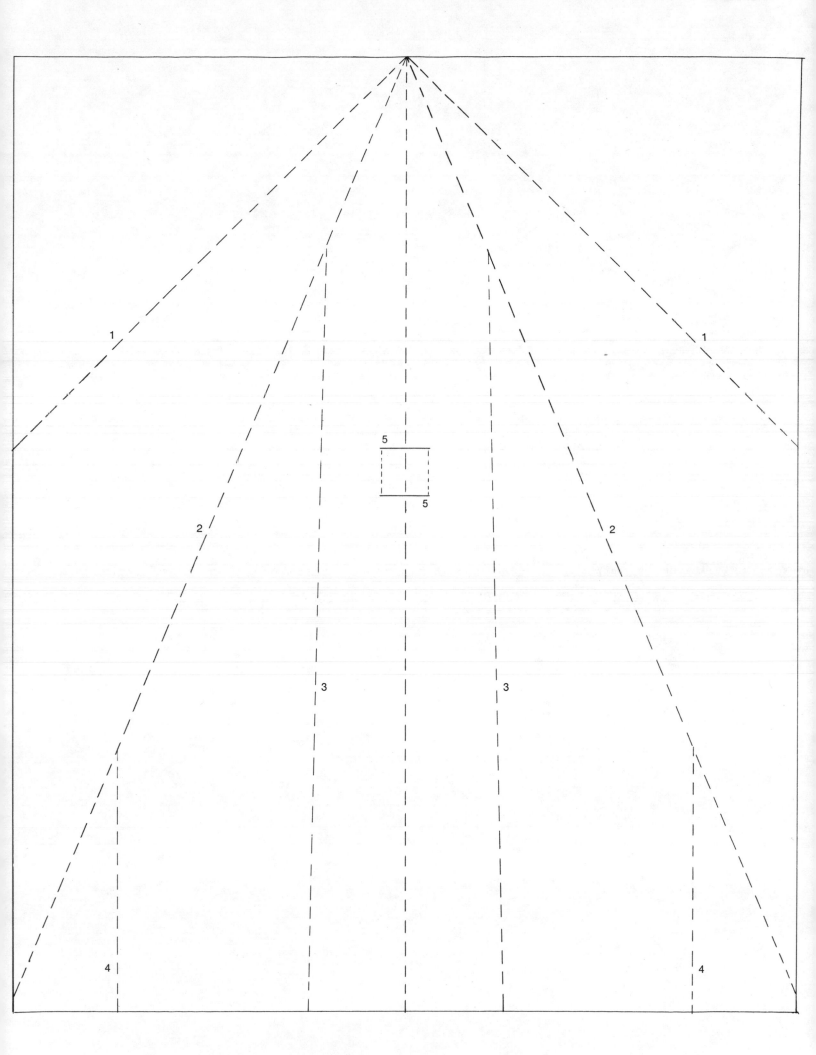

William C. Etherington
Englewood, Colorado
(*Martin Company*)

INSTRUCTIONS →

Cut out on all solid lines.
Starting from top, make overlapping folds
until you reach last dotted line 1.
Then fold up on center line
and down on lines 2 and 3. Tape fold
together at nose. Work line 4
to form upward curve. (See photo)

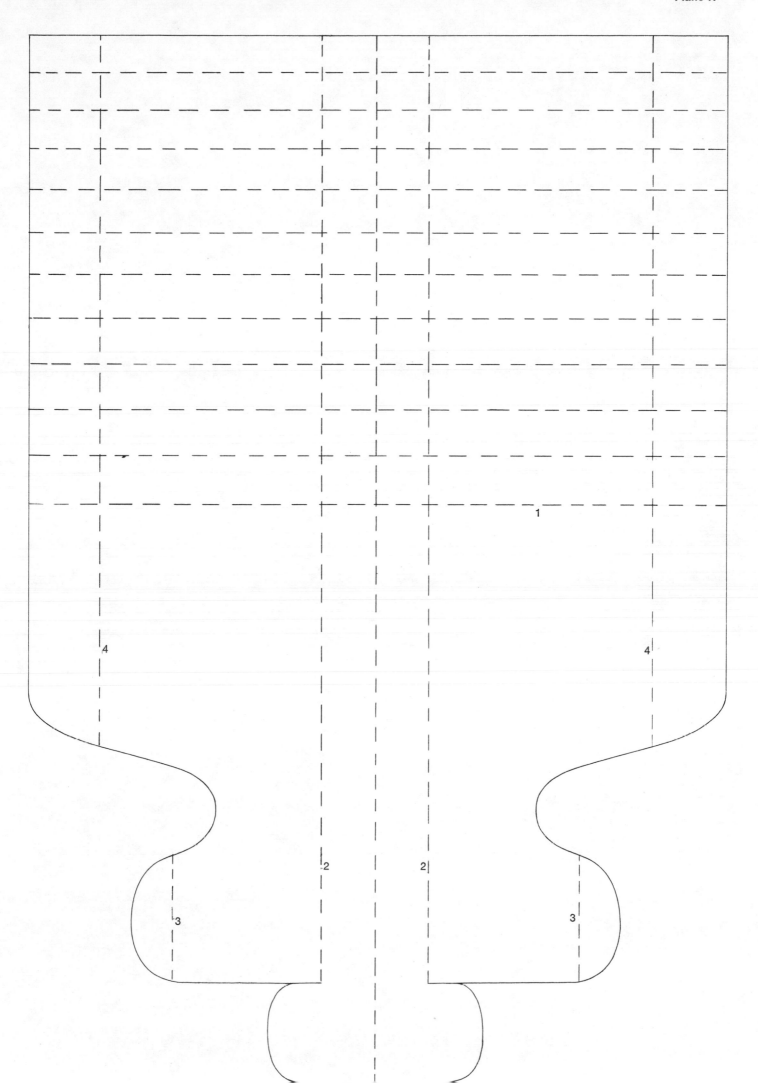

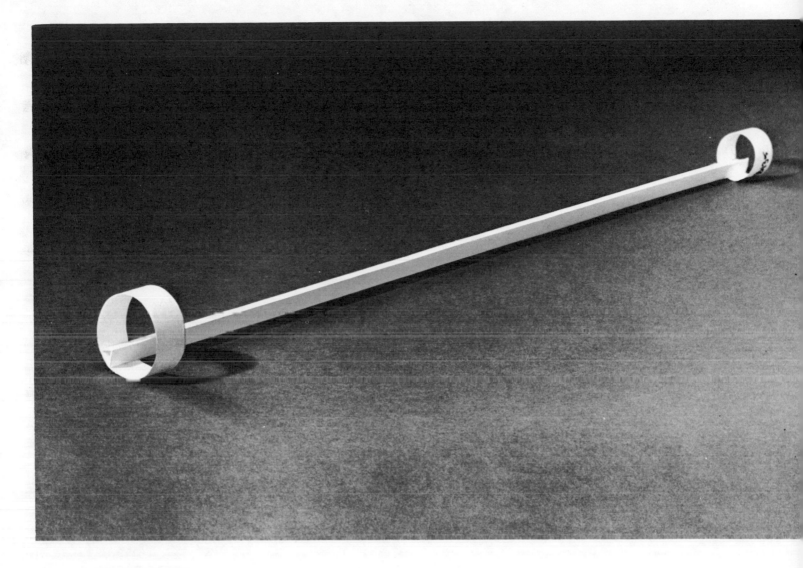

Philip W. Swift
Rochester, New York

INSTRUCTIONS →

1. Cut out A. Bring two ends together
   to form a ring. Overlap to dotted line
   and glue together

2. Repeat with B

3. Cut out C. Score along
   dotted lines. Overlap two sides and glue
   to form a triangular rod

4. Place each ring on ends of rod
   so that a flat side of the rod
   is glued to inside of ring.

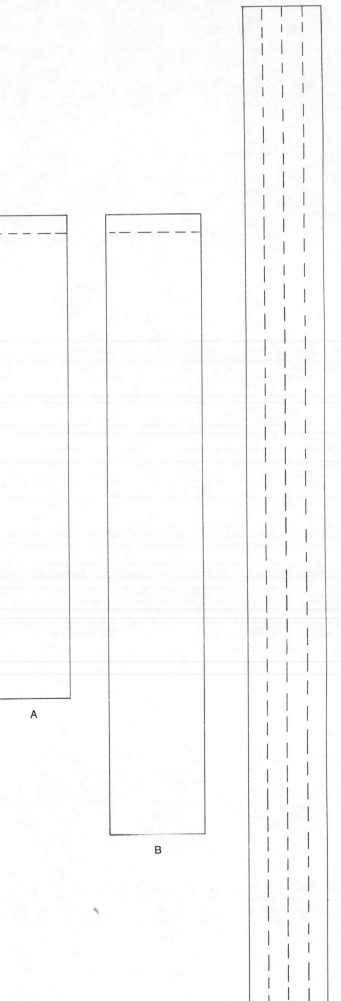

A

B

C

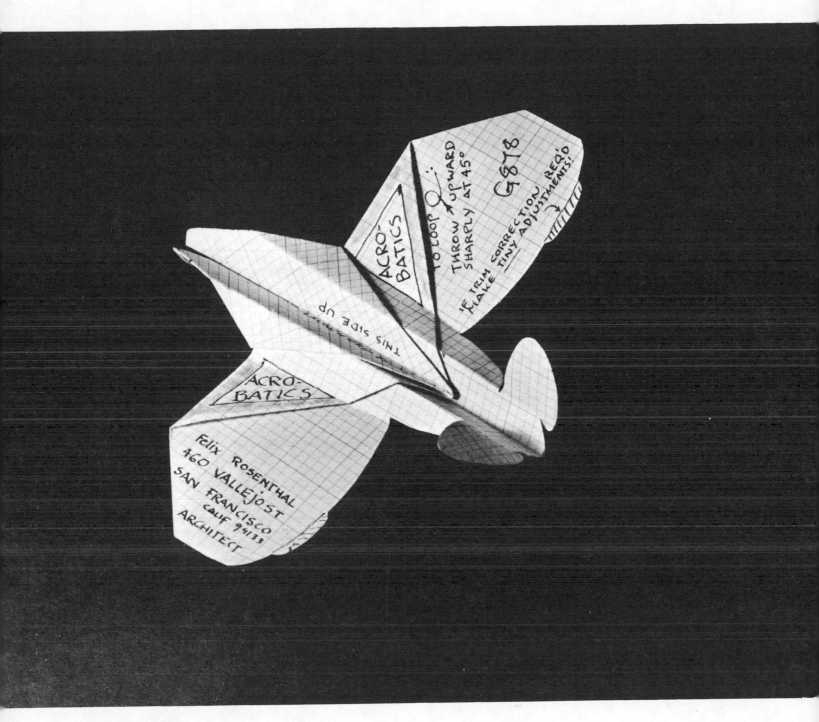

Felix Rosenthal
San Francisco, California
(*Architect*)

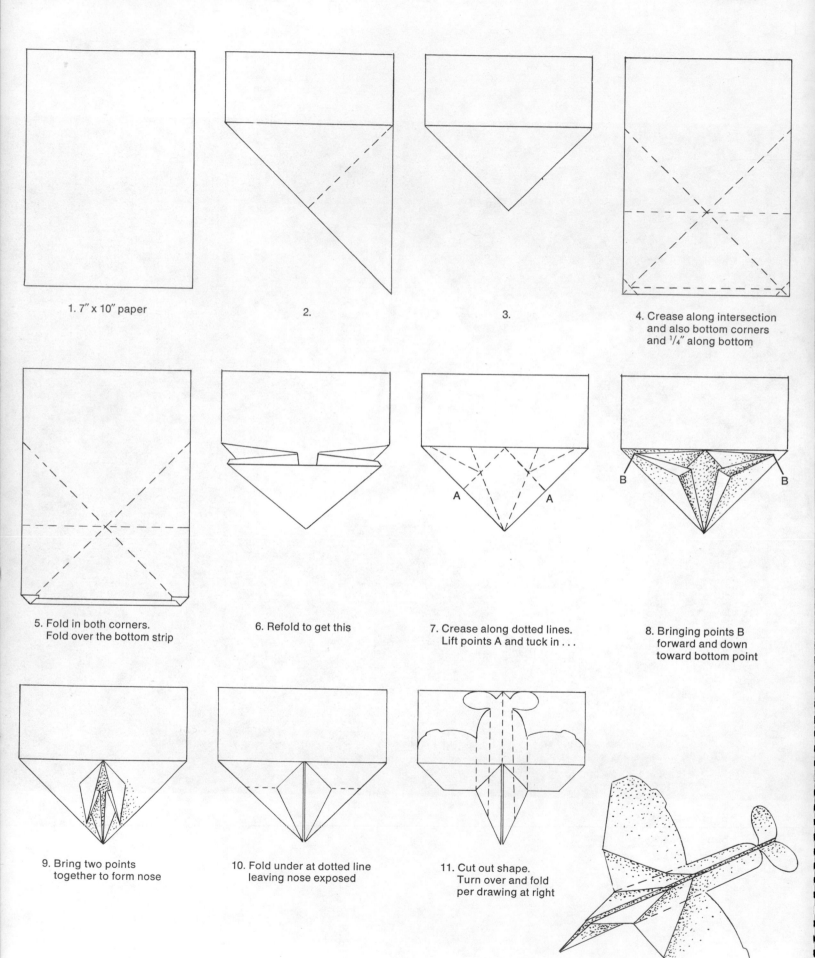

1. 7" x 10" paper

2.

3.

4. Crease along intersection and also bottom corners and ¼" along bottom

5. Fold in both corners. Fold over the bottom strip

6. Refold to get this

7. Crease along dotted lines. Lift points A and tuck in . . .

8. Bringing points B forward and down toward bottom point

9. Bring two points together to form nose

10. Fold under at dotted line leaving nose exposed

11. Cut out shape. Turn over and fold per drawing at right

Bend ailerons and elevators to suit

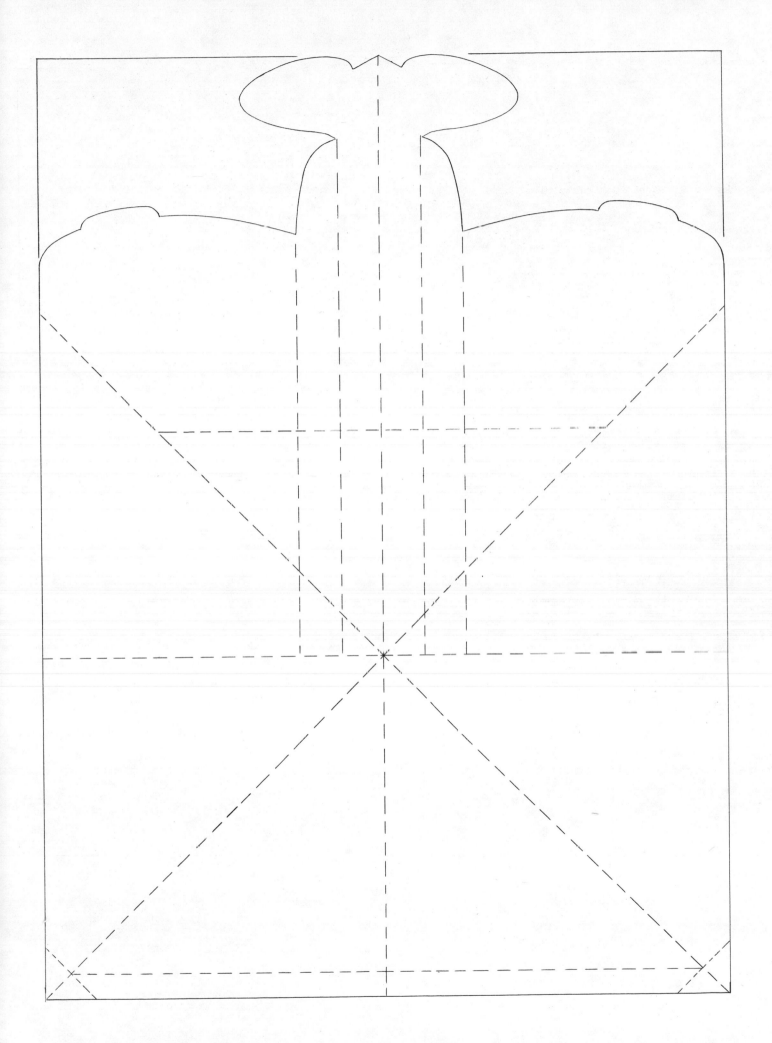

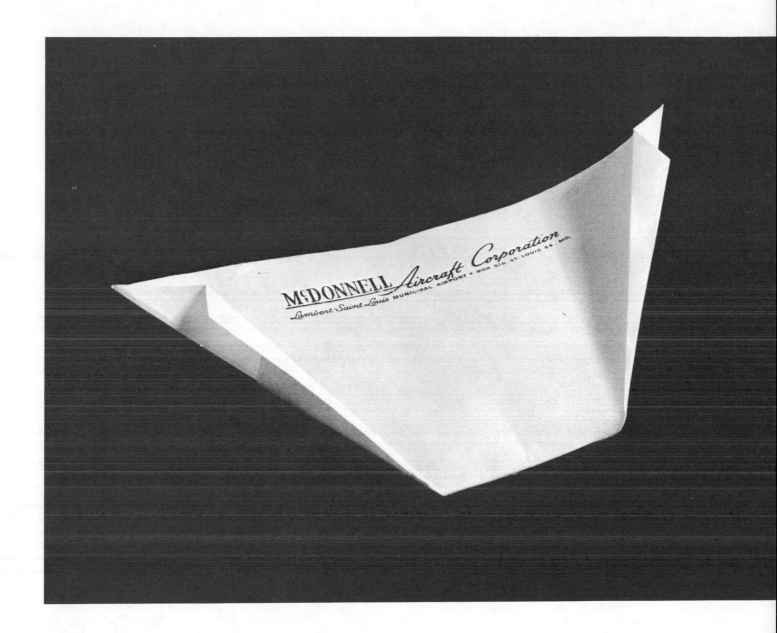

Irl R. Otte
St. Louis, Missouri
(*McDonnell Aircraft Corporation*)

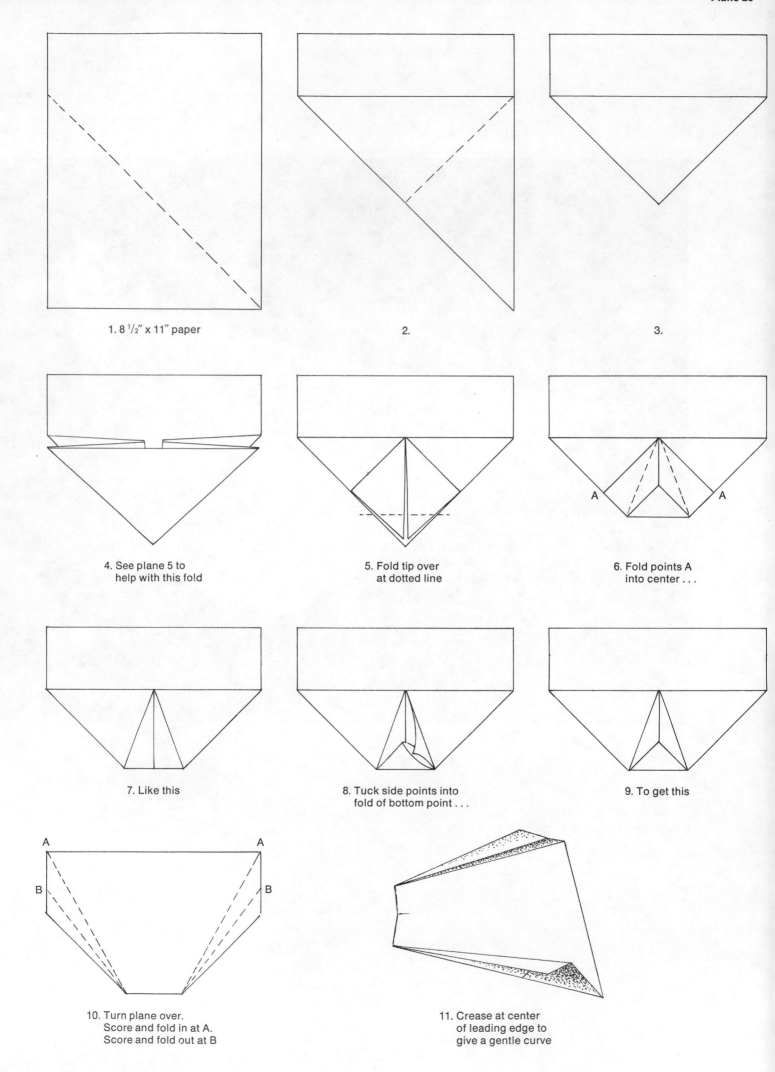

1. 8 ¹/₂″ x 11″ paper

2.

3.

4. See plane 5 to
   help with this fold

5. Fold tip over
   at dotted line

6. Fold points A
   into center . . .

7. Like this

8. Tuck side points into
   fold of bottom point . . .

9. To get this

10. Turn plane over.
    Score and fold in at A.
    Score and fold out at B

11. Crease at center
    of leading edge to
    give a gentle curve

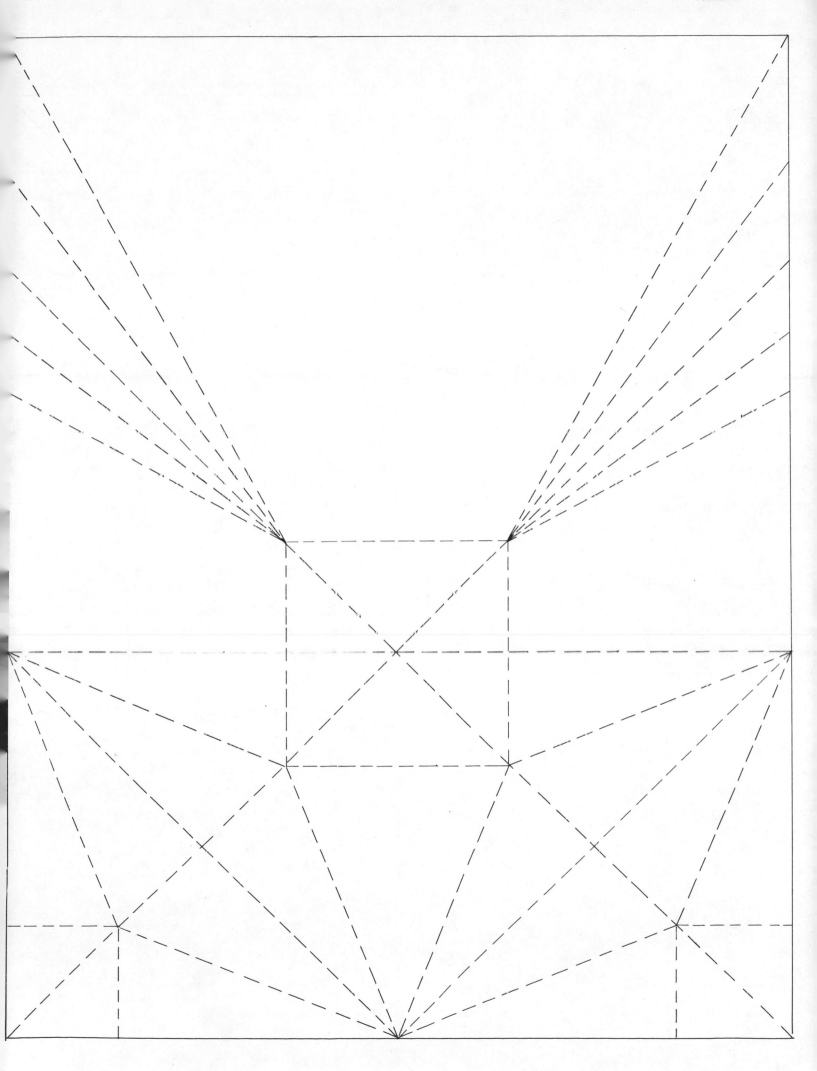

Epilogue

"WORKING AS an ordinary hand in a Philadelphia ship-yard, until within a few years, was a man named John L. Knowlton. His peculiarity was, that while others of his class were at the ale houses, or indulging in jollification, he was incessantly engaged in studying upon mechanical combinations. One of his companions secured a poodle-dog, and spent six months in teaching the quadruped to execute a jit upon his hind-legs. Knowlton spent the same period in discovering some method by which he could saw out ship timber in a beveled form.

"The first man taught his dog to dance. Knowlton, in the same time, discovered a mechanical combination that enabled him to do in two hours the work that would occupy a dozen men, by slow and laborious processes, an entire day. That saw is now in use in all the ship-yards of the country. It cuts a beam to a curved shape as quickly as an ordinary saw-mill saw rips up a straight plank.

"The same unassuming man has invented a boring-machine, that was tested in the presence of a number of scientific gentlemen. It bored at the rate of twenty-two inches an hour, through a block of granite, with a pressure of but three hundred pounds upon the drill. A gentleman present offered him ten thousand dollars upon the spot for a part interest in the invention, in Europe, and the offer was then accepted. The moral of all this is, that people who keep on studying are sure to achieve something."

—FROM AN ESSAY, "The Value of Brains," in the *Scientific American Reference Book,* 1876.